PROPHECY AND THE APOCALYPTIC DREAM

Prophecy and the Apocalyptic Dream

Protest and Promise

D. S. RUSSELL

HENDRICKSON
PUBLISHERS

ISBN 1–56563–054–8

Library of Congress Cataloging-in-Publication Data

Russell, D. S. (David Syme), 1916–
    Prophecy and the apocalyptic dream: protest and promise
  /   D. S. Russell.
        p.   cm.
    Includes bibliographical references and indexes.
    ISBN 1–56563–054–8 (pbk.)
    1. Apocalyptic literature—History and criticism.
2. Prophecy—Judaism.   3. Prophecy—Christianity.
I. Title
BS646.R88   1994
291.2′3—dc20   94-11229
                                                                        CIP

TABLE OF CONTENTS

PREFACE

Retirement, it has been said, is for younger people. True or not, I count myself fortunate to be able to devote more time to study and writing than was possible in more hectic days. The subject that has occupied most of my attention over the years has been that of Old Testament and early Jewish apocalyptic literature whose worth, I am convinced, has all-too-often been undervalued or even regarded as the domain of cranks and charlatans.

The focus of this small volume is not on the texts themselves but on their meaning and interpretation at the turn of the second millennium. The reason for this emphasis is, as I see it, the misuse to which scripture has sometimes been put by not a few writers whose interpretation, it would seem, has been too much influenced by speculation and subjective judgment and by ideological prejudice. My hope is that the criticisms I offer and the suggestions I make will be constructive rather than destructive and lead to a better appreciation of a form of writing that has a lot to offer in our understanding of the biblical record and the scriptural revelation.

Scripture references, where not otherwise indicated, are to the Revised Standard Version of the Bible.

I am indebted, as always, to my wife, not least for her patient endurance of my closed study door at a time of life when, I am assured, more relaxed and leisurely pursuits are called for! I am grateful also to the editor and staff of Hendrickson Publishers for their unfailing courtesy and their readiness to consider the publication of yet another of my periodic sorties into the apocalyptic world of myths and monsters.

Bristol
D. S. Russell
1993

INTRODUCTION

"SECRET" BOOKS

Within the Old and New Testaments there are a number of books and passages, chief among which are the books of Daniel and Revelation, that are generally designated by the words "apocalypse" or "apocalyptic." The Greek word *apokalypsis* means an "uncovering" or "unveiling," indicating something that has been hidden but has now been revealed. The definition of these words in this context will be considered later; here we simply note that the apocalyptic book, though often a hybrid form of writing and a complicated creature, claims to record the uncovering of "secrets" or "mysteries" long hidden from human eyes but now revealed to the privileged and inspired writer.[1] Some of

---

[1] For a description of these "mysteries" see M. E. Stone, "Lists of Revealed Things in the Apocalyptic Literature," in *Magnalia Dei: The Mighty Acts of God: Essays on the Bible and Archaeology in memory of G. Ernest Wright*, ed. F. M. Cross, W. E. Lemke, and P. D. Miller (New York: Doubleday, 1976) 414–52; and D. S. Russell, *Divine Disclosure:*

these "mysteries" have to do with "the secrets of creation"; most have to do with "the latter end of the days" when history, as it has been known, will cease to be and a new era of righteousness and peace will be ushered in.

What is perhaps not as well known is that, during the so-called intertestamental period (ca. 250 B.C.–A.D. 100), alongside Daniel and Revelation, there emerged in Palestine and in the Dispersion a veritable flood of books, not a few of which were of an apocalyptic kind that are of no small interest for the study of the Judaism of that time and for an understanding of the origins of Christianity. Among these, Daniel and Revelation rightfully hold pride of place. The extracanonical apocalyptic books were written, it would seem, by wise and learned people who sincerely believed they had an important message to pass on to their readers. Their actual readership would of necessity be rather limited; but as the number of their books grew, the influence of their teaching would extend much further afield than the books themselves. There is good reason to believe that, together with the book of Daniel itself, they were a source of great encouragement to faithful Jews who "looked for the redemption of Israel," but who were made to suffer in varying degrees, not only in the time of Antiochus Epiphanes during the earlier years of the second century B.C., but also during the uneasy years of the Hasmonean House (successors to the Maccabees), the oppressive years of the Herodian rulers, and the restrictive years of the Roman procurators which came to a head with the outbreak of the Jewish War in A.D. 66, culminating in the fall of Jerusalem in A.D. 70 and the end of the Jewish state. It is not surprising that in such circumstances these books, including those originally written in Hebrew and Aramaic,

An Introduction to Jewish Apocalyptic (London: SCM and Philadelphia: Fortress, 1992) ch. 5.

gained in popularity and were spread abroad in the common Greek language.

IN JUDAISM AND IN CHRISTIANITY

There is evidence to show that a number of influential "teachers of the Law" within Judaism were themselves influenced by the apocalyptic tradition, particularly in the period preceding the fall of Jerusalem in A.D. 70. But as time passed and as "official" or "normative" Judaism, with its emphasis on the centrality of the Law and "the tradition of the elders," gained in strength, the apocalyptic teaching largely fell out of favor and came in course of time to be regarded with suspicion and even with hostility by those in authority. Reasons for this are not difficult to find. The speculative nature of the apocalyptic hope sat uneasily with the assured teaching of the reformed Judaism of the time; the old spirit of nationalism and even fanaticism that had both fed and fed upon this style of writing was now seen to be inappropriate and even dangerous in the search for accommodation with the state. But alongside its challenge to rabbinic authority and the security of the state went another determining factor—the adoption and adaptation of the apocalyptic writings by the rapidly expanding Christian church. Christian apocalyptic writings began to appear, and existing Jewish works were revamped with Christian interpolations. The result was that the Jewish apocalyptic tradition has been largely preserved and perpetuated within the Christian tradition and disseminated by the Christian church, not least through the translation of these books into many different languages besides Greek—Latin, Syriac, Armenian, Ethiopic, Coptic, Slavonic, Georgian, and so forth—in which many of them have survived to this day.

Just as the apocalyptic tradition had become popular in Judaism in earlier times, so now it gained considerable popularity within Christianity. Once again the reasons for this are not hard to find. Their teaching fitted in with the hopes and expectations of the church and gave added authority to its message—their teaching concerning "the two ages," the imminent appearance of the Messiah and the messianic kingdom, the "woes" that would precede that great event, the final judgment, the resurrection of the dead, and the eternal destiny of the righteous and the wicked in the life to come.

But, as in Judaism so also in Christianity, reservations concerning this type of literature began to be expressed, no doubt for somewhat the same reasons: its highly speculative treatment of traditional Christian teaching, particularly in its reference to "the last things," and the embarrassment it caused vis-à-vis the state when, in course of time, the church came increasingly to be identified with "the establishment." This is no doubt reflected in the rejection as well as the rather reluctant recognition of books of an apocalyptic kind within the canon of scripture.

APOCALYPSES AND THE CANON OF SCRIPTURE

Eventually the two books of Daniel and Revelation were recognized as canonical, but their passage into the canon was in each case none too smooth.

In the case of Daniel two related questions have to be asked: Why did the rabbis, who were suspicious of the revolutionary use to which such writings could be put, unhesitatingly reject other apocalyptic works but accept Daniel? And why does Daniel appear in all the first-century sources and in the Greek, Latin, and succeeding translations as one of the four major prophets within the prophetic section of the canon, whereas in the Hebrew-Aramaic Bible it appears in that section known as "the Writings," the earliest literary evidence for its inclusion there being somewhere between the fifth and the eighth centuries? Klaus Koch, in a helpful essay,[2] has suggested an answer to both these questions—why Daniel was accepted as canonical scripture and why it was apparently relocated from the Prophets to the Writings during the early rabbinic period.

In reply to the first question he suggests that the rabbis accepted it as canonical because by that time the generally accepted interpretation of the fourth monarchy in Daniel 2 and 7 was that it referred to the Roman (not the Greek) Empire—an interpretation (not simply a reinterpretation) dating from at least the first century A.D. among Jews and Christians alike. The prophecy concerning the kingdom made of iron and clay that would be shattered (Dan 2:3) and the prophecy concerning the dreadful monster that would be slain (Dan 7:7) still awaited fulfillment and, in the rabbis' judgment, had to refer to Rome! "Thus," concludes Koch, "for the oppressed or even persecuted Jewish and Christian communities Daniel received an actualization beyond all other prophets. This unique significance offers a possible explanation for the strange fact that out of the rich religious literature of the late Israelite period (since 200 B.C.) only Daniel was commonly accepted as a part of the Holy Scripture."[3]

The answer to the second question concerning its transfer from the prophetic corpus to the narrative section of the canon, Koch further assumes, may be found in a shift

---

[2]Klaus Koch, "Is Daniel also among the Prophets?" in *Interpreting the Prophets* (ed. James Luther Mays and Paul J. Achtemeier; Philadelphia: Fortress, 1987) 237–48.
[3]Ibid., 246f.

of accent "from eschatology to pedagogics," from the prophet as "proclaimer of the coming kingdom" to "the preacher of repentance and the Torah."[4] Be that as it may, and for whatever reason, the book of Daniel, after grave hesitations, was incorporated into the canon of scripture and in its Greek version was thus interpreted within the Christian church for many centuries to come.

Within the early Christian church the book of Revelation likewise was not welcomed with unanimity. Its language, imagery, and graphic portrayal of great tribulations preceding "the last days" did not somehow square with the message of the Gospels and epistles with their emphasis on the efficacy of Christ's death and resurrection as God's saving acts in the redemption of the world. It must have seemed to many—for all its popularity in some circles—to be an alien book, out of keeping with the revealed good news that had "turned the world upside down." True, Paul in 1 Thessalonians and Peter in the second letter bearing his name gave expression to their expectations in apocalyptic terms, but their exposition and interpretation were on a different plane from that of John of Patmos.

And so recognition of Revelation as canonical scripture was slow in coming. "From the time of Dionysius of Alexandria (around A.D. 260), its integrity in the East was violently shaken. Only after Athanasius in his *Thirty-ninth Easter Epistle*, and the Latin Church under the influence of Augustine around the close of the fourth century A.D., accepted it in their canonical lists did it receive widespread sanction as a part of the New Testament."[5] Even long after this time it continued to be questioned, not least by Re-

---

[4]Ibid., 246.
[5]Hugh Anderson, "A Future for Apocalyptic?," in *Biblical Studies: Essays in Honour of William Barclay* (ed. Johnstone R. McKay and James Miller; London: Collins, 1976) 57.

formers like Martin Luther who recognized it as "neither apostolic nor prophetic."[6] But thankfully Revelation was not only included in the New Testament canon but has continued to enrich the Christian church and to inspire its ongoing witness with an unrivaled vision of the risen and returning Lord to whom God has already given the kingdom.

AN AMBIVALENT APPROACH

The contrasting reaction of "official suspicion" and "popular enthusiasm" shown to apocalyptic in the earliest days of the church has continued throughout the whole of its history. No doubt much of the caution displayed has come as a reaction against the excesses demonstrated from time to time by individuals and by "fringe" sects who have adopted a literalistic approach and have acted in such a way as to bring the Gospel into disrepute or else have steered the church into a collision course with the state.

This same suspicion has been shown, though for different reasons, in academic circles, particularly in the nineteenth and earlier part of the twentieth centuries. Thus, the apocalyptic literature has been described as "the product of weak minds" which "contaminated" the theology of Jews and Christians alike.[7] In more recent years, however, there has been a distinct change of attitude so that today, as perhaps never before, the value of the apocalyptic writings is being much more readily recognized by New Testament scholars and systematic theo-

[6]Ibid., 58.

[7]R. T. Herford, *Talmud and Apocrypha* (London: Soncino, 1933), and G. F. Moore, *Judaism in the First Centuries of the Christian Era* (3 vols.; Cambridge: Harvard University Press, 1927, 1930).

logians alike.[8] This rehabilitation of apocalyptic has been sufficiently well documented to require no further elaboration at this point.

Meanwhile, on the "popular" front, interest in prophecy and apocalyptic has continued unabated, in some sections of the Christian church at any rate, and, if anything, has become much more widespread in recent years. No doubt the times through which our present generation has been passing have been one significant factor in this regard, with its "wars and rumors of wars" and its threats of total extinction not just of individuals but also of the whole human race. Whatever the reasons for this renaissance (and they are diverse), great interest is being shown by literally millions of people, most of them in the United States. It is an interest very different from that shown in academic circles and concerns not so much the text and the circumstances that occasioned it as the interpretation of that text in terms of today's world, the impending "end" of history, and the beginning of a new creation. The keenest interest is shown by those who would call themselves "conservatives" or "fundamentalists" who adopt a literalistic approach to the interpretation of scripture and find in the prophetic and apocalyptic texts forecasts of the distant future and their fulfillment in the events of our own generation. Daniel of Babylon and John of Patmos are often presented as better soothsayers and more accurate prognosticators of the future than any clairvoyant or fortune-teller of today. Their books, though written 2000 or more years ago, are said to foretell the rise of Hitler and Stalin to power, to see clearly in advance the emergence and demise of Communism as a world power, to prophesy in precise detail the return of Israel to "the promised land," to

---

[8]See references to E. Käsemann, W. Pannenberg, and J. Moltmann in Russell, *Divine Disclosure*, xvii, and in Klaus Koch, *The Rediscovery of Apocalyptic* (SBT; London: SCM, 1972) 14.

pinpoint the date of the end of the world, to recognize the signs of the approaching battle of Armageddon and the second advent of Christ. The focus of such prophecies narrows down to our own day, giving a clear sign that the "end" is at hand and the kingdom of God is about to be ushered in.

THE PURPOSE OF THIS BOOK

The subject of this small volume is also the interpretation of prophecy and apocalyptic, and its focus is likewise on the fulfillment of scripture and its relevance for the days in which we are now living. Its approach, however, is very different from that of the literalist/fundamentalist which, in my judgment, is often much too arbitrary, speculative, and subjective. It is, I believe, a misuse of scripture to see in it some kind of cosmic horoscope or an Old Moore's almanac. Such an approach, as I understand it, is based on a false notion of what prophecy is and what the apocalyptic books were trying to say. This does not imply, however, that I am totally content either with a purely academic and "detached" approach which may well smack too much of the classroom and the cloister and perhaps makes too little attempt to listen to the voice of God speaking in it and through it. The apocalyptic message, when rightly heard, has indeed, I believe, a relevance for our own generation that is every bit as real and every bit as powerful as that of the "popular" approach.

In the pages that follow we shall look first at the nature of apocalyptic itself and the circumstances that occasioned it; we shall next examine some "popular" attempts at interpretation in terms of "predictive prophecy" with their proposed precise fulfillments in our own day; then in the final chapter we shall consider possible criteria of interpretation, based on the New Testament approach to the Old Testament, which may provide a better and safer basis and indicate at what points in the apocalyptic message we may find a word of hope for our own generation. Behind its often high-flown language, its esoteric symbolism and its mysterious allusions, the message of these books is in fact very much down-to-earth, written as it is by real people in real-life situations, and conveying a message that is much bigger than the times in which the authors were living. The books they produced and the message they proclaimed are worthy of our most careful consideration today.

1

PROPHECY AND THE APOCALYPTIC DREAM

A PERPLEXING LITERATURE

This small book is about the apocalyptic literature of biblical times of which the books of Daniel and Revelation are the best known examples. Its aim is to help the reader to understand what message such books may have, not only for the days in which they were first written, but also for these modern times.

STYLE AND CONTENT

The apocalyptic books (Daniel and Revelation are only two among many more, as we shall see) are not easy to understand either in their style of writing or in their contents. For the most part they describe the substance of dreams and visions ostensibly vouchsafed to some illustrious men in antiquity, sometimes mediated or interpreted by an angel, concerning the "mysteries" or "secrets" of the cosmos, the course of history, and the coming of God's kingdom. The reader is introduced to a transcendent world beyond this world of time and space where mysteries are made plain and the coming of "the end" is revealed. The style of writing is highly imaginative and often speculative, expressed in colorful imagery and symbolic language culled from different sources; apocalyptic also uses mythological figures from ancient traditions whose precise meaning is not always clear (see ch. 2).

The reader is led into a bewildering world of fantasy and dreams—weird and wonderful beasts the like of which the human eye has never seen, falling stars that take the shape of fallen angels, heavenly beings consorting with "the daughters of men," giant offspring from which emerge demons that inhabit the earth, mystical mountains, mysterious horsemen, monstrous births, devastating earthquakes, destructive floods, and ravaging fires that consume the ungodly. These and many other "woes" appear on the earth as a prelude to the coming day of judgment and the appearance of God or his Messiah in his fast-approaching kingdom.

MEANING AND INTERPRETATION

Establishing the meaning of such books within their own historical and cultural setting is difficult enough. Much more difficult is the attempt to see their precise relevance, if any, for the times in which we are now living. This, however, has not deterred some from making the attempt. Throughout the generations this area of investigation has become the "happy hunting-ground" for many kinds of "seekers after truth" and has attracted perhaps more than its fair share of cranks and even charlatans. This is not to deny the sincerity and integrity of many others whose Christian devotion and love of scripture are beyond dispute, who find in the biblical apocalypses and related prophecies a word from God which is apposite to the world of this generation. It has to be confessed, however, that in not a few cases—not least in recent years—the interpretations offered have been so subjective and speculative that they leave themselves open to the charge of misrepresenting and even abusing scriptural truth.

I have no desire to attack those who follow such a path, many of whom are no doubt good and godly men and women; but there is need, I believe, to guard against interpretations which may not, for all their sincerity, ring true to the biblical revelation itself. I trust that what I write will be with due modesty and restraint, yet with a firmness which rises out of a desire to maintain the integrity of scripture.

Modern speculation of the kind indicated often finds expression in the production of diagrams and charts indicating predetermined eons and "dispensations" into which, it is believed, history has been divided by God as a prelude to the coming of "the end" and the dawning of God's kingdom. Reference is made, for example, in excited tones to the "Rapture" when "the saints" will be caught up to meet their Lord in the air; the fearful battle of Armageddon, which must be fought before the second advent of Christ, occupies an important place in this scenario; the talk is of premillennialism and postmillennialism and the catastrophic and devastating end of the world at a precise date and in the precise circumstances foretold in scripture (see ch. 3). At other times the speculation identifies people and places mentioned in scripture with present-day rulers and contemporary nations or world events. By such means predilections and prejudices can readily mingle with propaganda to distort the text to make it fit in with the writer's theological or political stance. This is all very popular stuff. It is a stance that I for one utterly reject and it is to counteract this kind of approach that this small volume is written—not so much by attempting to disprove or discredit what is being said as by presenting what I hope is a more balanced account and a more acceptable method of interpretation.

THE VOICE OF PROTEST

We shall see presently that the apocalyptic literature had a "mixed parentage" and reflected in its growth a wide variety of historical circumstance. The long period between the fall of Jerusalem in 587 B.C. and its capture by the Romans in A.D. 70 showed many fluctuations in Israel's fortunes. It began in the despondency of the exile, continued under the authoritarian rule of foreign powers, and ended in catastrophe. The pressures under which the Jewish people had to live during that time were well-nigh insufferable. It is perhaps hardly surprising that, in such circumstances, the voice of protest began to be heard, and men and women began to "see visions and dream dreams" of better days to come when God himself would intervene and bring about his salvation. And so it was that with the protest went the promise that, despite all that individuals and nations might do, God's purpose would at last be fulfilled and his kingdom come.

The nature of the protest no doubt varied with changing circumstance, but three "pressure points" can perhaps be identified which closely intermeshed with one another: a "lost" world and a corrupt society, the encroachment of Hellenism whose pervasive influence had seeped into the soul of Judaism and done much to destroy its very life, and the experience of oppression and persecution, not least under the Syrian tyrant Antiochus IV Epiphanes.

A LOST WORLD AND A CORRUPT SOCIETY

The fall of Jerusalem in 587 B.C. was a traumatic event for the whole Jewish people. The exile in Babylon was a day of deep darkness, penetrated only by the light that came from such prophets as Ezekiel and the writer of Isaiah 40–66. Nor were the immediate postexilic years much better. They were, for many of the returned exiles and their descendants, years of disillusionment and despair. The social order, such as it was, seemed to be collapsing around them. The course of justice was being perverted on every side; corruption had entered into business dealings and even into the law courts; violence was abroad in the land, and people did not know where to turn for justice and security.

> Justice is rebuffed and flouted
> while righteousness stands at a distance;
> truth stumbles in court
> and honesty is kept outside (Isa 59:14 REB).

Hopes were high that the rebuilding of the temple and the rehabilitation of the cult would bring with it the rich blessing of God. But affliction followed affliction; the people continued to languish, and injustice prevailed. The situation was made even worse, it would seem, by rivalries that developed within the priesthood, leading to enmity and even excommunication (cf. Isa 65:5). The offended party, critical of the "establishment," looked more and more to the intervention of God to deliver them and their people from the impasse to which they had come.

In such circumstances, and as time went on, the oracles of the prophets, with their promise of God's deliverance, came to be carefully collected and preserved. They offered the promise of a new day, the day of the Lord, that would bring devastating judgment on the nations and effect deliverance for God's own people Israel. The "messianic age" would at last dawn, and Israel would enter into its glorious heritage. But when? In this day of darkness it must have seemed to many that not only was the voice of prophecy dumb, but that God himself was dead! The mood of the moment is well expressed by the Psalmist in these words:

> We cannot see any sign for us,
> we have no prophet now;
> no one amongst us knows how long
> this is to last (Ps 74:9 REB).

Into such a world came the forerunners of those we know as the apocalyptists. With clear voice they protested against the wicked world around them which seemed past redemption:

> The earth itself is desecrated by those who live on it,
> for they have broken laws, disobeyed statutes
> and violated the everlasting covenant (Isa 24:5).

So critical had the situation become that God himself must intervene—not in some far distant time, but now! The day of the Lord was on the way. He was about to execute judgment on the earth! There was no future for the world as it was; the time had come for him to make an end and a new beginning. The promise of God made through the prophets would indeed be fulfilled. The hour of judgment and of deliverance was close at hand.

Their protest, then, carried with it a promise that was more than merely wishful thinking and more even than a sincere affirmation of faith; it was nothing less than a divine revelation that God was indeed about to do a new thing.

The Encroachment of Hellenism

The world the apocalyptists protested against had been shaped by many factors; a major one was the pervasive influence of Hellenism, a culture adopted by Alexander the Great and sponsored by him and his successors. Hardly anyone was able to escape its influence—even those devout Jews from whose ranks the apocalyptic writers themselves came. But to them it represented a way of life in so many respects diametrically opposed to the faith of their forebears.

The new "enlightenment" which Hellenism introduced, they were convinced, was a deadly danger, especially because it had such a strong drawing-power for the young. Its democratic form of government, its aesthetic appreciation, its unabashed delight in the shape and movement of the human body, its encouragement of science, philosophy, and the liberal arts, its irresistible charm and irrepressible vitality—all these made a powerful appeal that passed its own judgment on the rather frumpish and stuffy Judaism of temple, synagogue, and law-observance.

But if the up side of Hellenism was dangerous, its down side was more dangerous still. To the pious Jew it represented a corrupting and degenerate influence that issued a challenge to social ethics and religious practice alike. Immorality and vice were prevalent, gluttony and drunkenness were commonplace. This culture that was the pride of Hellenism had a subculture that contained within itself the baneful seeds of corruption. And what affected social life affected religious life as well; in such a society these two could hardly be separated from each other. Participation in athletics or attendance at the theater, for example, involved, if not actual sharing in heathen rites, then implied recognition of foreign gods. Hellenism moreover, as it developed, acquired more and more a syncretistic content in which the occultism of the East, with its superstitious and magical overtones, intermingled with the "wisdom" of the West.

It is small wonder that voices of protest were raised among the Jews against this insidious danger to all that they held dear. Among these protesters were the Hasidim, the "pious ones," who were to play a part in the Maccabean revolt. They were men dedicated to "the Law of Moses," who probably belonged to the ranks of the scribes (cf. 1 Macc 7:12) with priestly connections. It has been argued by some that it was from their ranks that the author of the book of Daniel came. Be that as it may, the apocalyptic writers obviously shared in the protest. The promises made by Hellenism, they believed, were utterly false and quite indifferent to the corruption that lay at its roots and would inevitably bring about its destruction. Their own promise was altogether different: God himself would intervene in judgment, cleanse the world of evil, and restore the fortunes of his people Israel.

OPPRESSION AND PERSECUTION

A third "pressure point" leading to protest on the part of the apocalyptists was the oppression and persecution of the Jewish people, especially in the practice of their religion. Not all the apocalyptic books arose in this way, but some did. The outstanding example of this is the book of Daniel in the time of Antiochus IV Epiphanes (175–163 B.C.).

The story of Antiochus and the ensuing Maccabean revolt is too familiar to require more than the briefest reference here. Pressure on the Jews became insufferable, and the time came when protest exploded into open rebellion. Political oppression was followed by religious persecution. The holy temple was desecrated and the sacred altar defamed; religious rites were forbidden and the sacred Torah proscribed. It was as if the Jews of this second century B.C. were being plunged into the darkness of the sixth-century exile, to suffer all over again cruel subversion to an alien power. The book of Daniel, with its stories of faithfulness and valor and its visions of the ultimate triumph of God's kingdom, was not only a protest against the tyranny of the king, but a promise that the day was coming when the rule of "monsters" would come to an end, and God's rule would begin on the earth. The kingdom, the dominion, and the power would be given to his people and that right soon!

But no sooner had that crisis passed than others followed, first under the Hasmoneans (successors to the Maccabees) and then under the Romans and their appointees, right up to the fall of Jerusalem in A.D. 70. Apocalyptic is a literature of crisis to which it responded with confidence and courage: evil could not and would not prevail. True, the promises made by the prophets had not yet been fulfilled and the hopes of people like Daniel had not yet been realized. But these were simply promises postponed and hopes deferred. The great day was surely coming and was coming soon! Their protest, then, was much more than a wringing of hands and a cry of despair; it was an affirmation that God was sovereign ruler over earth and heaven and would deliver up the kingdom to "the saints of the Most High."

PROPHECY AND APOCALYPTIC

There has been much debate among scholars concerning the precise origins of apocalyptic, in particular whether it is to be traced back to prophecy or to the wisdom tradition and to what extent it was influenced by scribal wisdom of a divinatory kind that owed much to ancient Babylonian thought. The content of that debate need not concern us here.[1] Whatever other influences there may have been, it seems clear that Old Testament prophecy featured fairly prominently in its development. This is not to say, however, that there were no great differences between them, some of which can be briefly mentioned here.

SPOKEN WORD AND WRITTEN BOOK

There are distinct differences, for example, in their style of presentation. The canonical prophets, on the one hand, were essentially preachers, whose oracles might subsequently be put into writing either by themselves or by

---

[1] For a summary of this debate see Russell, *Divine Disclosure,* 19ff.

someone else; with what they believed to be God-inspired authority they declared, "Thus says the Lord." The apocalyptists, on the other hand, were essentially writers, bidden by God to record what they had seen and heard in secret books which would thereafter be kept hidden until their disclosure at the time of "the end." The fact that these books were now being disclosed was a sure sign that "the end" was at hand. With conviction to match that of the prophets, they too made known their message with an authority they believed to be God-inspired. They lived at a time, as we have seen, when it was "officially" believed that, ever since the time of Ezra the prophet, the voice of prophecy had been dumb and that prophecy itself was dead. They did not claim for themselves the title of "prophet"; nevertheless, they believed themselves to be the prophets' true heirs, sharing their inspiration and declaring, as they had done, a God-given message to their generation.

Moreover, whereas the prophets made known their message in their own name, the apocalyptists hid themselves behind their books, which, more often than not, they wrote pseudonymously in the name of some ancient worthy in Israel's history whose very antiquity lent authority to their own books.

Apocalyptic, then, is essentially a literary phenomenon, though many of its concepts and beliefs were no doubt part of a fairly long oral tradition, gleaning its contents from many fields of religious thought. To say this, however, is not to imply that it is to be dismissed as something quite artificial or contrived. There is reason to believe[2] that behind the literary expression and literary convention there may well have lain, in not a few cases, a profound personal visionary experience that would, as in the book of Daniel, move the recipient deeply both emotionally and even

---

[2]See D. S. Russell, *The Method and Message of Jewish Apocalyptic* (London: SCM and Philadelphia: Westminster, 1964) 164ff.

physically (cf. Dan 8:17f.). A graphic description of this is given in the pseudepigraphical work, 4 Ezra 14, where the visionary writer tells how he had fallen into a trance in which he was possessed by the spirit of God, enabling him to record all the sacred books, canonical and noncanonical alike, that had previously been destroyed by fire. Such experiences remind us of the ancient shaman more than they do of the canonical prophet, with the sole exception perhaps of Ezekiel, who shows certain shaman-like qualities and in this respect may be regarded as a "throwback" to those ecstatic prophets we read of in Israel's earlier history.

PREDICTION AND ITS FULFILLMENT

It has often been said that the prophets, in their proclamation, dealt with the present, not with the future, and so their message consisted in forth-telling, not in foretelling. This, however, is only a half truth and as such is misleading. It is true that their message dealt with the present—with contemporary personal and social morals as well as with national threats to Israel's security from surrounding nations. But it would be wrong to think of them as simply erstwhile journalists, observing and recording changes in the moral climate of society, fluctuations in the national crime rate, or trends in international politics.

Their prophecies in fact dealt with the future as well as the present. Foretelling took its place alongside forth-telling and formed an important element in the prophet's mission. Quite frequently the prophet would express God's condemnation of sin, for example, in the form of a general principle that judgment would indeed follow. At other times a prophet would go much further and proclaim the occasion of that judgment and even identify the agent through whom it would be inflicted. Prophetic predictions, moreover, were not just haphazard; to the prophet the course of history was a consistent revelation of the mind of God who would not be turned aside from his purpose by any person or nation. Because of this, there was an inevitability about history and about future events. They were conditioned and determined, it is true, by human conduct; but they remained within God's control. It was the prophet's high privilege, as one permitted to stand in the heavenly council (cf. 1 Kings 22:19ff.; Isa 6:6ff.; Jer 23:18ff., etc.), to be witness of these divine secrets, and it was correspondingly the prophets's great responsibility to make known the predictions thus revealed. Amos, for example, is able to say, "Indeed, the Lord God does nothing without revealing his plan to his servants the prophets" (3:7 REB). This ability to predict future events was popularly felt to be a guarantee of the prophet's dependability and gave proof that God was with him. Indeed, it was believed that the successful operation of this power was a necessity for the fulfillment of his ministry and was a test for judging which was a true and which a false prophet: "When a word spoken by a prophet in the name of the Lord is not fulfilled and does not come true, it is not a word spoken by the Lord. The prophet has spoken presumptuously" (Deut 18:22 REB).

It is true, then, that the predictive element is to be found in the prophetic utterance and that unfulfilled prophecies constitute a continuing problem for the devout Israelite as well as for the prophet. Nevertheless, it remains true that the chief emphasis is on the events of the prophet's own day and God's judgment upon them. "The business of the prophet," writes Robertson Smith, "is not to anticipate history, but to signalize the principles of divine grace which rule the future because they are as eternal as Yahweh's purpose. True faith asks nothing more than this. It is only unbelief that inquires after times and seasons."[3]

---

[3]W. Robertson Smith, *The Prophets of Israel* (2d ed.; London: A. & C. Black, 1907 [1895]) 249.

When we turn to the apocalyptic writers we find that the predictive element is much more prominent than it is in the prophets—or so it would appear to be. This qualification is added because of the device of pseudonymity through which the writer, in the name of an ancient worthy, "predicts," sometimes in some detail, the events of the passing generations between that worthy's day and the time of the writer. Usually the prediction given of the period that remains, from the writer's own day onwards, is both brief and in general terms and refers to "the end" that is at the point of taking place.

We observe too that the element of predetermination of events is much more clearly defined than it is in the prophets. History is here divided into precise periods of time, predetermined by God, in which thrones and kingdoms are seen to rise and fall by the will of God. The few remaining years before "the end" are in God's hands, as are all the rest, and will most surely witness his triumph and that of his people in the coming of his kingdom when he and they will rule and put all enemies under their feet. In such predictions of predetermined history the readers can recognize the various stages which it has passed through and identify the precise point that God's overall plan has reached in their generation. They can see that there is not long to wait before the great denouement takes place, before the cosmic drama of all the ages will reach its fitting climax, and "the end" will come.

In this dramatic scenario unfulfilled prophecies play a significant part in charting and interpreting the course of events. Perhaps the best known example of this is in Jeremiah 25:11f., 29, where it is said that Israel's captivity will last for seventy years. This date had long since passed, and true deliverance had not yet come. The writer of Daniel comes to the rescue (cf. 9:24): the interpretation, he says, is that deliverance will come after seventy "weeks of years," i.e., 70 times 7 = 490 years, bringing the period of waiting down to the writer's and the reader's own day in the second century B.C. This was not just a reinterpretation of the prophecy, but the true and indeed only interpretation, the one intended from the beginning. It is a method of interpretation that is continued and finds new applications in other apocalyptic books also, even within the book of Daniel itself (cf. 12:11f.), and has been perpetuated down through the centuries until our own day.

The same can be said of the use made by the apocalyptic writers of numbers in general. They loved to juggle with figures and with number patterns which they used as a means of forecasting the future and in particular the time of "the end." Behind this practice no doubt lay the belief, common in the ancient world, that within the concept of number was concealed the mystery and meaning of the cosmos itself. The apocalyptic writers seem to have been fascinated by the subject and adapted it to serve their own ends in charting the predetermined course of history and in predicting its consummation in the coming of God's kingdom and "the age to come." It is perhaps small wonder that in due course the rabbis came to refer to them rather disparagingly as "calculators of the (messianic) end" whose predictions led only to frustration and disillusionment when the time predicted at last arrived and the Messiah had not yet come. But the apocalyptists were not to be put off. Frustrated forecasts led to revised predictions. It is a saga that has been repeated in almost every generation since then and is not uncommon still in our own day. "Hope springs eternal in the human breast"—and numerology gives it that extra boost!

If the interpretation of prophecy, then, is bound up with numerology, numerology in turn is bound up, in the apocalyptists' mind, with astronomy and astrology, which help them to understand the life of the cosmos and to forecast the end of history. In the apocalyptic writings (some more than others) frequent reference is made to the order and movement of sun, moon, and stars. The Book of Heavenly Luminaries (1 Enoch 72–82), for example, describes the movement of the sun through its twelve "portals," the phases of the moon, and the way taken by the stars, all of them governed by predetermined laws which will have no variation until the day of judgment. So too in the book of Jubilees where it is said that Enoch records "the signs of the heavens according to the order of their months" (4:17), corresponding to the signs of the zodiac. In these writings, however, we can detect a marked ambivalence in this regard. In some apocalyptic books (for example, those in the Enoch and Moses traditions) such matters have a great fascination; astrology is actually traced back to its origins in Father Abraham. In others they are regarded with great suspicion and seen as a betrayal of trust in God. Such fascination has, of course, continued to this day, not so much in religious circles as in the popular imagination and in the popular press where trust in the stars and the signs of the zodiac to forecast the future have all too often replaced trust in a living God.

THE MESSIANIC HOPE

We have seen, then, that there are some distinct differences as well as similarities between prophecy and apocalyptic in respect of their method of presentation and the "techniques" they adopt. The same can be said about the message they proclaim, not least that concerning "the messianic hope" enshrined in the so-called messianic prophecies that point forward to God's deliverance of his people from all ills and all oppression and to a time when he will establish his royal rule over all the earth.

The prophets in their day were not slow to condemn their own people and to castigate them for the moral and social evils they had committed. They called them to repentance, holding over them the dire threat of judgment if they failed to turn from their evil ways. But their message was not all "doom and gloom." They assured the people that the God they worshipped was indeed a merciful God who was ready to forgive and would deliver them from the hand of their oppressors and from everything that would enslave. Such a hope had early beginnings in Israel's history, but it was the experience of the exile that gave it new impetus. Sometimes it was to come through the agency of "the Lord's anointed," the "messiah," and at other times by the direct intervention of God himself. Judgment would fall on their enemies, but Israel would be saved.

Such a vision of the future is a marked feature of much of the exilic and postexilic literature of the Old Testament. An idealistic picture of the future is painted in which the golden age will have come for Israel, and the whole earth will have been transformed. So marvelous are God's works that they cannot be adequately expressed in plain prose but require the colorful language of poetry and the symbolic language of myth (see pp. 47ff.).

Of particular interest are oracles contained in Isaiah 40–66 and others embedded like precious stones in earlier prophecies. When God's day of deliverance at last comes:

> The eyes of the blind will be opened,
> and the ears of the deaf unstopped.
> Then the lame will leap like deer,
> and the dumb shout aloud (Isa 35:5f. REB).

Even the parched wilderness will "burst into flower," and

> waters will spring up in the wilderness,
> and torrents flow in the desert (Isa 35:6 REB).

The old order of things will completely pass away and there will be a new creation in which humans and beasts, earth and heaven, alike will share. This is expressed nowhere more graphically and nowhere more lyrically than in Isaiah 65:

See, I am creating new heavens and a new earth . . .
I am creating Jerusalem as a delight,
and her people as a joy . . .
The sound of weeping, the cry of distress
will be heard in her no more . . .
My people will not toil to no purpose
or raise children for misfortune . . .
The wolf and the lamb will feed together
and the lion will eat straw like the ox,
and as for the serpent, its food will be dust.
Neither hurt nor harm will be done
in all my holy mountain
(Isa 65:14ff. REB).

This prophetic message of the golden age to come is taken up with enthusiasm by the apocalyptic writers who in the process stamp their own distinctive marks upon it. The prophetic hope becomes the apocalyptic dream. At the risk of oversimplification we may identify these distinctive marks in four key words: universality, transcendence, dualism, and resurrection.

Universality

It is true that prophets like Amos and the writer of Isaiah 40–66 proclaimed in their day the universality of God's sovereign rule. Under his control he had not only Israel, but all the other nations of the earth. Their belief in the unity of history was a corollary of their belief in the unity of God himself.

The apocalyptic writers shared this same belief and in the process widened its scope and brought new religious insights to bear upon it. Past, present, and future were all seen as one, governed, controlled, and determined by the irresistible purpose of God. Ages past, like the time to come, were part of the overall plan of God that embraced the present time with its troubles and afflictions. God, as ever, was still in control.

And as with history, so also with creation. The prophet of the exile had spoken of "a new heaven and a new earth."

But the cosmological unity that the apocalyptists envisaged went far beyond anything that the prophets had foreseen. Heaven and earth, sun and moon, stars and planets—all were under the sway of the one sovereign Lord. Historical unity and cosmological unity were partners in declaring the universal rule of him who was sovereign over all created things.

Transcendence

To the apocalyptic writer, moreover, the God of history and creation was also the God of "the last things." To the prophet the phrase "the latter days" meant some point of deliverance in Israel's near or distant future; to the apocalyptist the phrase "the latter end of the days" had a quite different focus demonstrating a transcendent quality that went beyond anything the prophet had ever contemplated. The kingdom of God came within the orbit of history, and yet to the apocalyptist it transcended history and assumed a cosmic dimension. History would come to a close; the present world order would cease and be replaced by one of an essentially different kind. Evil powers—no longer simply foreign tyrants and foreign armies, but cosmic agencies—would be overthrown. God would bring deliverance, and the whole earth would be cleansed. "In the mystery to come," writes the author of the Qumran book of Mysteries, "wickedness shall retire before righteousness as darkness retires before the light and as smoke vanishes and is no more; so shall wickedness vanish for ever and righteousness appear like the sun" (1QMyst 1). Such hopes had, of course, found expression in the prophets, but now in the apocalyptic writings they became more and more transcendent, with increasing emphasis laid on the supernatural and the supramundane (see ch. 2).

Dualism

This brings us to the third key word, dualism. Here is something that has no parallel in the prophetic writings. "The

Most High," says the writer of 4 Ezra, "has made not one age but two" (7:50). Over against "this present evil age" is set "the age to come." Only a short time remains, for "(this) age is hastening swiftly to its end" (4:26). Evil and corruption of all kinds will be done away; the wicked will face most awful judgment; Satan and his demon hordes, who are in control of this present evil age, will be "bound hand and foot and thrown into the darkness" (1 Enoch 10:4). The righteous, on the other hand, will escape the great judgment that awaits the wicked; they will inherit the blessings of the age to come in which will be "neither weariness nor sickness, nor affliction nor worry, nor want nor debilitation, nor night nor darkness . . . but they will have a great light" (2 Enoch 65:7ff.). Such cosmic dualism is a marked feature of these writings and goes far beyond anything to be found in the prophetic books.

Resurrection

As in the prophets so also in the apocalyptists, the blessings God has prepared for the golden age to come are corporate in nature—they are for "the righteous" and for "Israel," and judgment is reserved for "the wicked" and for "the nations of the earth." But here in the apocalyptic writings, alongside this emphasis, stress is laid on the destiny of the individual. Beyond this world is another world, and beyond this life is another life in which the individual will receive due recompense—the wicked with torments indescribable and the righteous with resurrection life and the bliss of heaven. Here is something the prophets did not foresee, though they hoped beyond hope for the vindication of their people and that of God himself. The apocalyptists saw that vindication in a life beyond death when the righteous (and in some cases the wicked also) would be raised in resurrection to receive their appropriate reward.

By such means as these, then, the apocalyptic writers followed up the "messianic oracles" of the prophets and proclaimed to their troubled times a message of hope in the midst of despair. God would indeed deliver his people, and the time of that deliverance was near. The apocalyptic dream was no mere mirage, but a spring of living water in a dry place, not just for the Jewish people in their times of persecution, but in due course for the Christian church as well.

THE APOCALYPTIC LITERATURE

But what are these "apocalypses" and this "apocalyptic literature," and where did they come from? It is generally recognized that the expression "apocalyptic literature" does not refer to any one literary type but includes the "apocalypse" and other distinct literary genres such as testaments and prayers which belong to the same milieu and share the same characteristics and motifs.

The words "apocalypse" and "apocalyptic" are notoriously difficult to define.[4] Suffice to say here that the "apocalypse" is generally recognized as a distinct literary genre with a particular interest in "heavenly secrets" (made known to a visionary by means of dreams and visions or by the agency of angels) as these affect the life of the cosmos, the course of human history, the destiny of the world, and the future of individuals within it. The word "apocalyptic," as already noted, can be applied to other related literary genres besides that of the "apocalypse." Together they show a peculiar interest in "the last things" and the final judgment, although their concern is wider than simply that of eschatology.

---

[4]See further, *Apocalypse: The Morphology of a Genre* (Semeia 14; ed. J. J. Collins; Missoula: Scholars, 1979) 9, and Russell, *Divine Disclosure*, 8ff.

OLD TESTAMENT ORIGINS

Equally difficult is the question of apocalyptic origins and their relation to Old Testament prophecy. There is much to be said for the claim that, embedded in the prophetic writings (even in preexilic books such as Isaiah, Ezekiel, and the Twelve Prophets), we can trace an "apocalyptic re-working" of earlier prophecy that was believed to contain secret knowledge of God's future judgment of Israel and the nations. Elsewhere, in Isaiah 40–66 for example, the way was also being prepared for the birth of an apocalyptic-style literature which was to develop over the following centuries. In describing this development P. D. Hanson uses such expressions as "proto-apocalyptic" (Isaiah 40–55), "early apocalyptic" (Isa 24–27, 34–35, 60–62; Zech 9–10), "middle apocalyptic" (Zech 12–13), and "full-grown apocalyptic" (Isaiah 56–66; Zech 11). I myself prefer not to categorize the writings concerned in this way, but would borrow an analogy from human biology and regard them as "embryonic apocalyptic." Even at such an early stage they are beginning to develop the form and appearance of the "full-grown child," which was reached around the beginning of the second century B.C. and indeed somewhat earlier in books like Daniel and 1 Enoch (in part). The development and growth of this "child of prophecy" can be traced particularly through Isaiah 24–27 ("the Isaiah Apocalypse"), Zechariah 1–8 and 9–14, and Joel 3–4 which, together with Ezekiel 38–39, give a preview, as it were, of what was yet to be.

A prominent theme in these passages is the destruction of Israel's enemies and the restoration of God's people. In Ezekiel 38–39, for example, we have two parallel accounts of terrible devastation in which we hear resounding echoes of the prophetic day of Yahweh, a concept that no doubt lies behind the apocalyptic final day of judgment. The nations that attack Israel are under the command of

"Gog of the land of Magog," a mysterious figure whose origins are likely to be found in mythology rather than in history. (Elsewhere, as in Genesis 10:2, 1 Chronicles 1:5, and Revelation 20:8, Magog is also named as a person.) He will be dragged away, like some great sea monster, with hooks in his jaws (cf. 38:3), recalling the old Babylonian dragon myth (see pp. 47ff.) that reappears in later apocalyptic writings. The figure of Gog epitomizes a force of evil in the world that is more than simply one of military might; it is a mysterious manifestation foreshadowing the concept of cosmic evil to be found so prominently in certain later apocalyptic books.

Further "foreshadowings" of apocalyptic appear in Zechariah 1–8 where again the Gentiles epitomize evil and are destined to be destroyed. Israel's victory will be a prelude to the golden age promised of old. In particular, we observe that the visions received by the prophet, with their vivid imagery and fantastic symbolism, are a familiar motif in apocalyptic writings. We note too the interest shown in angelology and the role played by Satan, both of which are of significance in the religious thought of the apocalyptic books.

Zechariah 9–14 (by a different hand from that of the earlier chapters) continues the same theme of Israel's triumph over its enemies and goes on to describe Yahweh's defense of Jerusalem and the coming of the "messianic age." David's line will be restored and Yahweh's kingship acknowledged throughout the earth.

So too with Joel 3–4 where the day of Yahweh is given great prominence as a day of destruction and abject terror. Here, more clearly than in any of the other writings, we have indications of what were to become features of apocalyptic—the outpouring of the spirit of prophecy, supernatural portents on earth and in the skies with "blood and fire and columns of smoke" (2:30), the assembling of the nations for judgment, and the return of God's people to their own land.

The writer of Isaiah 24–27 likewise gives a graphic description of God's judgment falling on the peoples of the earth. The earth itself will be split asunder and turned upside down (24:1), and the sun and moon will be darkened (24:23). There will be a massive cosmic catastrophe in which even "the host of heaven" will not escape punishment (24:21). This will be followed by a "messianic banquet"—another feature which appears in the apocalyptic books—in celebration of the dawning of the "messianic age." In 26:19 reference is made to the resurrection of the righteous who will share in the blessings of the age to come. If this is a reference to the resurrection of individuals and not, as in Ezekiel 37, to that of the nation as such, then it is the earliest allusion of its kind in the Old Testament and once more points forward to a belief which was to be fostered and nourished in the apocalyptic tradition.

This cursory glance at these writings shows "embryos" at different stages of development, soon to come to birth. The period of gestation was long and arduous, but in due course apocalyptic, the "child of prophecy," was born. The earliest biblical book that can be so designated is the book of Daniel, which first saw the light of day in troubled times.

THE BOOK OF DANIEL

The "apocalypse," and indeed the apocalyptic literature as a whole, is the offspring of "mixed parentage." If its mother is prophecy, its father may be claimed to be the wisdom tradition, which itself is of mixed lineage! The offspring of this "mixed marriage," like the children of any family, differ greatly from one another. This can be seen fairly clearly when we compare, say, 1 Enoch with the book of Daniel. The former "takes after" its father and indulges in much speculation such as is to be found in wisdom

writers of that period; the latter owes much also to its
father, but it takes after its mother more than does 1 Enoch,
showing much greater interest in prophetic insights like
those contained in Ezekiel and Jeremiah. It has been described, along with others, as a "horizontal apocalypse" in
the sense that it is concerned with the course of history and
its end, over against others designated "vertical apocalypses," which are characterized by the seer's transportation in vision to the ends of the earth and into heaven itself
where the mysteries of the cosmos and the abode of angels
are disclosed to him. The author of Daniel makes use of
dreams and visions to uncover heaven's secrets, which for the
most part relate to the predetermined course of history and
its denouement with the coming of God's eternal kingdom.

At this point we may note a divergence of judgment
between conservative scholars and others concerning the
date of the book and, as a consequence, the nature of the
prophecy it contains. The former take it at its face value and
argue that it was written during the time of the Babylonian
exile in the sixth century B.C.; the author was one, Daniel,
a Jewish exile, whose prophecies related, not to his own day,
but to the far distant future and to the fate of nations and
peoples many centuries after his own day. As a Christian
broadsheet has recently put it: "That which Daniel prophesies 2,600 years ago is now a reality. Nothing will prevent
it being fulfilled."[5] Such fulfillment is envisaged in terms of
the political upheavals of our own time and is a sign that
"the end" is near. Other scholars (and I venture to count
myself among them) would argue strongly for a date
around the year 165 B.C. in the time of Antiochus IV
Epiphanes, the Syrian ruler. The symbolic language used by
the writer to describe these events is only lightly veiled so
that it is possible to see in the several allusions clear refer-

---

[5]*Link-up* 176 (February, 1993).

ence to the events of Antiochus' own day and to identify his cruel attacks on the Jewish people and their religion that are known to us from other historical records of that time. The arguments in favor of such a date for the book as it now stands have been presented in many introductions, commentaries, and essays and need not concern us here in any detail. The most plausible explanation of its origins, in my judgment, is that the stories contained in chapters 1–6 concerning a Jewish exile and his three companions, and told for the most part in the third person, were current in the sixth century B.C. and handed down, probably by word of mouth, before taking their present written form and being joined with the visions contained in chapters 7–12 around the year 165 B.C. This would help explain why the stories do not reflect an era of severe persecution such as we find in the visions. These visions are, again for the most part, presented in the first person and form a unity with the narratives in the earlier chapters.

On this reckoning, the authorship is pseudonymous, the book being written in the name of some ancient worthy and the prophecies being "prophecies after the event," the author identifying himself with the sixth-century hero of the stories. On such an interpretation the writer's visions are not to be taken as prognostication of events many thousands of years later or as relating to the coming of God's kingdom in some far off time, but are to be seen as a reference to the troubled times in which the author was living and to the breaking in of God's kingdom which would for ever destroy the power of evil that tormented God's people Israel. It has to be remembered that pseudonymity (see p. 20) was a commonly accepted literary device at that time among others besides the Jews, which carried with it no hint of dishonesty on the part of the writer, but rather was an indication that what was written was backed by antiquity and that the words carried an authority that was more than simply make-believe. I would

thus refute the suggestion that the adoption of pseudonymity is in any way a denial of the veracity or authority of
scripture.

There is no extant evidence for such an exile as Daniel
in Babylon at this time outside the book of Daniel itself.
There is, it is true, reference to an otherwise unknown priest
of that name in Ezra 8:2 (cf. Neh 10:6), but this obscure man
can hardly be the source of such stories as we find in the book
of Daniel. Of greater interest are the references in Ezekiel
14:14, 20, and 28:3 and elsewhere (cf. the Ugaritic Tale of
Aqhat dating from the fourteenth century B.C.) to an ante-
diluvian hero called Daniel who is praised for his righteousness and wisdom. The indications are that from an early time
there was an ancient legend about a man called Daniel who
was regarded as a man of great renown. There is no proof
that the hero of our book is in any way related to this
legendary figure, but the evidence we have would appear to
point in that direction. The "Additions to Daniel," contained
in the Apocrypha, and the discovery of fragments among the
Dead Sea Scrolls referring to an individual bearing a resem-
blance to Daniel are a further indication that there may have
been a cycle of tradition concerning such a person which was
wider than the book of Daniel itself. Such findings enhance
rather than impoverish the witness of this intriguing book
whose message, while rising out of the circumstances of the
second century B.C., finds an echo in every generation and
not least our own; it is a message of encouragement and hope
in the midst of trial and despair.

EXTRABIBLICAL APOCALYPTIC LITERATURE[6]

The book of Daniel may have been the only "fully-
fledged" apocalypse to be accepted by Judaism as canonical

---

[6]See George W. E. Nickelsburg, *Jewish Literature Between the Bible and
the Mishnah* (London: SCM and Philadelphia: Fortress, 1981), and D. S.
Russell, *The Old Testament Pseudepigrapha* (London: SCM, 1987).

scripture, but it was by no means the only writing of its kind belonging to the "intertestamental" period. Having in mind the great interest shown in the figure of Enoch and the manner of his departure from this life (cf. Gen 5:24), it is not surprising that in due course there grew up an "Enoch tradition" with apocalypses associated with his name. One such is 1 Enoch (or the Ethiopic book of Enoch, having come down to us chiefly in an Ethiopic translation), a composite work in five parts, ranging from perhaps the third century B.C. to the first century A.D. These constitute five separate books: the Book of Watchers (1–36), the Book of Parables or Similitudes (37–71), the Book of Heavenly Luminaries (72–82), the Book of Dream Visions (83–90), and the Book of Admonitions (91–105 within which is the Apocalypse of Weeks, 93; 91:12–19), together with a conclusion (106–108). It is now generally recognized that the earliest sections (the Book of Watchers and the Book of Heavenly Luminaries) are pre-Danielic and are to be dated probably in the third century B.C. or even earlier. Both are marked by extensive cosmological speculation and in this respect are different from, say, the Apocalypse of Weeks and the Book of Dream Visions, which seem to have been written at the time of the Maccabean revolt and have a historical rather than a cosmological interest and in this regard have more in common with the book of Daniel than with the earlier Enoch apocalypses. There has been much debate among scholars concerning the date of the Book of Parables, which contains important references to the "Son of man." It may belong to about the middle of the first century A.D.

The contents of 1 Enoch are too diverse to describe even in outline here, and readers are recommended to read the text for themselves. It is a very different book from that of Daniel, showing much interest in cosmology, astronomy, and calendrical calculations, and paying much less attention to eschatology. First Enoch and Daniel, then, illustrate the wide range of religious interest within the

diverse apocalyptic literature at this time. Besides 1 Enoch
and Daniel, several other apocalypses are to be noted:

Second Enoch (the Slavonic Book of Enoch), perhaps
to be dated in the late first century A.D., describes the ascent
of Enoch through the seven heavens to the throne of God
and shows a dual interest in cosmology and eschatology. In
the longer of the two editions that have come down to us,
the seer passes through an eighth and ninth heaven where
the twelve signs of the zodiac are stored and finally to the
tenth heaven where he beholds "the Lord's face . . . ineffable, marvelous and very awful" (22:1).

The Apocalypse of Zephaniah (first century B.C. to first
century A.D.?) also depicts a seer who is taken on a cosmic
journey through the heavens where he is shown, in a series
of seven episodes, the glories of heaven and the torments
of hell. The prevailing theme is that of the judgment of the
ungodly.

The Apocalypse of Abraham (first to second century
A.D.), especially chapters 9–32, is of particular note. Once
more the seer is carried up to heaven where he beholds
many "great things" and from where he can see the earth
and its inhabitants and the judgment to come upon them
because of their idolatry. The present age—the last of
twelve "periods" into which history is divided—is nearly at
its close. Soon will come the final judgment; the Gentiles
will be punished, and God's "chosen one" will come to
gather together his scattered people and restore the sacred
temple.

Fourth Ezra 3–14 (=2 Esdras in the Apocrypha) and
2 Baruch are to be dated around A.D. 100. They reflect the
travail of God's people, the Jews, following the capture of
Jerusalem in A.D. 70 and seek to justify God in his dealings
with them. They speculate on the nature of the coming
kingdom, the world to come, and the destiny of people and
nations. They are particularly concerned about the problem of evil and the related problem of suffering, which the

fall of Jerusalem had exacerbated. The solution is to be found in the eschatological hope that the time is coming when the wicked will be punished, the righteous rewarded, and God's promises to Israel will at last be fulfilled. The Messiah, says Baruch, will come and establish his kingdom for ever.

Besides these apocalypses, there are other books which belong to the same milieu and reflect the same world view and so come within the scope of the term "apocalyptic literature," even though they represent different genres of literature than that of the apocalypse proper.

The book of Jubilees (second century B.C.) is a "running commentary" on Genesis and part of Exodus and is concerned with biblical laws, rites, and ceremonies. It has much in common with the Qumran literature and stands as a bulwark against the encroachment of Hellenism. It divides history into predetermined periods measured by "jubilees" (7 sabbatical years, or 49 years). The writer is not particularly interested in eschatology and has a conception of the "messianic kingdom" very different from the catastrophic event often described elsewhere. Of particular interest is its teaching concerning angels and demons and its dualistic presentation of a confrontation between the spiritual forces of good and evil.

The Testaments of the Twelve Patriarchs (second century B.C.), in its present form, shows clear Christian influence, but in its Jewish emphases shows an affinity with the book of Jubilees. It consists of a number of "testaments" in which two things are particularly stressed: ethical exhortation and eschatological expectation. The second of these finds focus in the persons of Levi and Judah who will effect salvation in the last days. Fragments of a Testament of Levi have been found at Qumran, where the patriarch, like the seer in the other apocalyptic writings we have examined, ascends in vision through the seven heavens where, among other things, he sees preparations already being made for the day of judgment and is confronted by the glorious throne of God. On returning to earth he is to declare God's mysteries among humankind (2:10).

The Testament (Assumption ?) of Moses (first century A.D.?) describes the history of Israel from the time of entry into Palestine to the time of the end. Moses prophesies the return of the exiles after a time of great apostasy, which is also a time of great suffering for God's people and in which the reader is able to recognize the apostasy under Hellenism and the suffering of faithful Jews in their own day. This suffering will hasten the coming of God's kingdom that will appear throughout all creation; the devil will be defeated and Israel will be raised to "the heavens of the stars" (10:9).

In the Testament of Abraham (first to second century A.D.) Abraham is told of his pending death and asks that first he be allowed to see "all the inhabited world" (9:6A). He is lifted up by cherubim and soars over all the earth. So enraged is he by what he sees of the wickedness of humankind that he calls down judgment from heaven which God in his mercy stays. He is then taken on a tour of heaven itself where he sees the places of judgment. He is shown a narrow way and a broad way along which the souls of men and women must pass. Their trial is to be by fire and by the balance at the hands of three judges: Abel, Israel, and God. He is told that intercessory prayer will avail much and so is encouraged to pray for the repentance of evil doers. On returning to earth he prepares to meet the fearsome Angel of Death and is carried off to heaven.

To this list must be added certain documents and fragments from among the Dead Sea Scrolls that have added to our understanding of such literature. There is no clear evidence that the Qumran Community actually produced apocalypses of their own; but the discovery there of no fewer than seven different manuscripts of Daniel and portions of ten Aramaic manuscripts of parts of 1 Enoch indicates clearly their deep interest in literature of this kind.

This is underlined by the presence of yet other apocalyptic-style writings, presumably produced at Qumran itself—the book of Mysteries, a Description of the New Jerusalem, an Angel Liturgy, the Genesis Apocryphon, and the Prayer of Nabonidus. Here we have a community that, in its own writings and in others that it cherished, shared in many ways the apocalyptic outlook and stood in the apocalyptic tradition.

The "apocalyptic literature," then, did not belong to any one cohesive or identifiable group, nor did it represent a common theological outlook. What the writers had in common was a world view, built no doubt on the prophetic witness of the Old Testament, but going well beyond it, not least in their understanding of the relation between the natural order and the supernatural (see ch. 2). They believed the "changes and chances of this mortal life" were to be understood in the light of that "other world" whose mysteries they had been privileged to behold.

THE BOOK OF REVELATION

The book of Revelation stands firmly within the apocalyptic tradition and draws freely on the concepts and imagery familiar to us from the other apocalyptic books. It is the only apocalypse per se to be included in the New Testament canon, though the apocalyptic influence is to be found throughout, in Gospels and epistles alike (see ch. 4). It shares much, then, with the Jewish apocalyptic books, but at least two distinguishing factors mark it out from these others.

One is that there is no need for the writer to adopt a pseudonym. He openly identifies himself as "(God's) servant John" (1:1). The book's authority is to be found, not in some long line of tradition going back to an illustrious figure in antiquity; but rather in the very revelation made known to him, both in its source (God himself speaking through his Son) and in its content (its "testimony to Jesus," 1:9). This "testimony" is not just the personal record of a private experience; it is a prophecy he shares with others of like mind who also witness to the truth of God as it is in Jesus.

Herein lies the second distinguishing factor—its witness to Jesus Christ the Son of God. Jesus the Messiah is not the military warrior or the fire-breathing "man from heaven" of Jewish apocalyptic; he is "a Lamb with the marks of sacrifice on him" (Rev 5:6 REB)—a picture altogether unlike any in the other apocalyptic books. This transformation in the portrayal of the Messiah reflects a like transformation in the character of the kingdom: it is the kingdom of the crucified and risen Messiah, to be entered through faith in him.

John's book arose out of circumstances not unlike those facing the Jews in the time of Antiochus IV Epiphanes. They were days of grave persecution for the Christian church, and these chapters were written to bring strength and encouragement in a time of great trial. They were written, moreover, in "the language of apocalyptic" with great effect, the language of symbolism so graphically expressed in the Jewish apocalyptic writings: secret books, ferocious beasts, mysterious numbers, and so on. Here too we find motifs familiar to us from those others: transportation into heaven, the glorious throne of the holy God, the "woes" that are to precede "the end," Satan and his demonic hordes overthrown, cosmic conflict on a massive scale, the delights of heaven and the dark recesses of hell, the final judgment, the conquest of evil, and the coming of the kingdom—a kingdom that is eternal in the heavens as a climax to a millennial kingdom here on earth. But these symbols and motifs are not the center of interest in this book; its focus from first to last is the glory of Christ who, as the crucified and risen Jesus, will reign supreme over all the earth and even now is crowned sovereign Lord. It is all too easy to dismiss this book as bizarre and alien to the "simple gospel" of Jesus of Nazareth and to fail to see the great depth of spiritual insight it contains and the sheer conviction therein that kept the faith of God's people alive in days of terrible persecution.

It is this setting and this insight, then, rather than its symbolism and imagery that make Revelation so relevant and so powerful in the message it still proclaims in our own day. It speaks with complete assurance of Christ's triumph in the very midst of the struggle. It addresses to real people in real-life situations a word from God, which is understood best perhaps by those who themselves have passed through the fiery trial. "The Apocalypse," writes Allan Boesak, "can only really be understood in its political and historical context. Both by the first readers and by the authorities of the time, this book was seen as a document with tremendous political implications. . . . To read it differently, as purely foretelling the future or as spiritual escapism into the eschatological world of monsters, dragons and mysterious numbers, is to misread it—indeed to distort it."[7]

Perhaps it was, partly at least, because it was "too political" that grave hesitations were expressed concerning its acceptance within the canon of scripture in the first place. Thankfully, as with Daniel, it has been preserved as scripture and has proved to be a source of enormous strength to many generations of Christians, not least our own. Its mixture of politics and paradise is not as strange as it might at first sight appear to be. In the apocalyptic books, and not least in the book of Revelation, we have a mingling of the natural and the supernatural which is surely a reflection of the incarnation itself. To that aspect of the apocalyptic vision we now turn.

---

[7]Allan Boesak, *Comfort and Protest: Reflections on the Apocalypse of John of Patmos* (Edinburgh: Saint Andrews and Philadelphia: Westminster, 1987) 32.

2

THE NATURAL AND THE SUPERNATURAL

HEAVEN AND EARTH

The apocalyptic writers were profoundly aware of being surrounded by an "unseen world" which might break in upon them at any moment through the medium of dreams and visions or in the person of an angel sent from heaven. In this, of course, they were in harmony with the Hebrew tradition of the Old Testament where God spoke to his servants the prophets by dreams and visions and invited them to stand in his heavenly council (cf. 1 Kings 22:19ff.; Job 1:6ff.; Isa 6:6ff.); angels appeared to them as messengers from God (cf. Gen 19:1; Zech 1:8ff.) and for those who had eyes to see, the angel hosts were all around (cf. 2 Kings 6:17). Their focus, however, was somewhat different from that of the prophets; it was to the supernatural world rather than the natural world they looked for the fulfillment of their hopes and dreams.

COSMIC UNITY

The world view they inherited was that of a two-tiered universe of earth and heaven. But separate though they were, they nevertheless formed a cosmic unity in which each part was vitally related to the other. Only when seen together could either part be understood. The earthly and the heavenly, the natural and the supernatural, were essentially one. They impinged on each other in such a way, for example, that angels might appear on earth as humans; earthly events were to be understood in terms of their heavenly counterparts; the coming kingdom, though established on earth, would display the transcendent qualities of heaven. So intermingled were the life of earth and the life of heaven that mortals, even here and now, could share the eternal life of heaven (cf. 1QH 3.18–23) and after death participate in it to the full and become like the very angels in heaven.

PRIVILEGED VISIONARIES

The God whom the apocalyptists worshipped was "the High and Holy One," "the Lord of spirits," raised high above the earth and seated on his glorious throne, "insulated" by myriads of angels who, as heavenly messengers, carried people's prayers to him and his replies to them. He was the ineffable God, enshrined in blazing light, whom no mortal dare approach.

And yet this same God had deigned to make known his divine "secrets" to a chosen few, a spiritual elite, who were given insights that other less privileged mortals could never hope to experience—insights into the meaning of the cosmos and the "signs of the end" when history would reach its glorious climax in the coming of the kingdom of God. By means of dreams and visions, these "chosen few" were permitted, as we have seen, to visit the ends of the earth and even to enter into heaven itself,[1] and from that vantage point to see the world as it really was and as it would one day become. Earthbound mortals could see only half the picture. To see things as they really were they had to see them whole, and this required the perspective of heaven. Heaven, with its divine mysteries, held the key to earth's mysteries, and these God in his goodness had chosen to make known.

Such knowledge, however, was not to be discovered by human ingenuity or wisdom, but only by divine revelation, and that wisdom from above. As Daniel says to Nebuchadnezzar:

> He gives wisdom to the wise
> and knowledge to those that have discernment;
> he reveals deep mysteries;
> he knows what lies in darkness . . . (Dan 2:21f. REB).

But Daniel makes it equally plain that what matters is not his own native ability or any wisdom he may possess more than others to see the workings and the ways of God; what really matters is the divine wisdom and God's readiness to make his secrets known (cf. Dan 2:30).

These dreams and visions, by means of which such disclosures were made, were not, as we might say, simply "subjective" reflections or subconscious imaginings; they did not simply "arise" out of a vivid imagination; they "fell" from heaven itself, conveying a message from God which was as "objective" and real as any brought by an angelic messenger straight from the divine presence.

These divine mysteries, then, containing "the secrets of all the ages," the recipients were commanded to record and seal up in their secret books, to be preserved until "the time of the end," so that "the wise" among the people might read and understand.

---

[1]For a more detailed examination see Russell, *Method and Message of Jewish Apocalyptic*, 164ff., and *Divine Disclosure*, 75ff.

THE SYMBOLIC LANGUAGE OF MYTHOLOGY

But how were such mysteries to be expressed? The apocalyptic writers were only too well aware that to describe the supernatural in words required more than formal prose; it required rather the imagery, the symbolism and the language of poetry. For this purpose they had a language "ready-made." The language of mythology they both adopted and adapted to suit the purpose in hand.[2] They adopted it from the complex culture of their own day, including that of the Old Testament which in turn had already adopted it from other cultures and traditions. And in the process they adapted it as a vehicle of the new revelations they had received.

There were two such myths ready-to-hand which they found particularly useful: what we might call the monster myth, reflected in the early chapters of Genesis, and the cosmos myth, reflecting other ancient cultures such as that of Mesopotamia and embodied in the Hellenistic culture of their own day.

THE MONSTER MYTH

IN GENESIS AND ELSEWHERE IN THE OLD TESTAMENT

Behind the creation story recorded in the book of Genesis, we can detect traces of an ancient combat myth, of which the apocalyptic writers in turn made good use. It appears elsewhere also in the Old Testament and in other more primitive traditions such as those of Canaan and Babylonia. It describes a struggle to the death between the creator and a great sea monster which appears in different

---

[2]See D. S. Russell, "Interpreting Scripture: myth and re-mythologizing," *ExpT* 104 (12, 1993), on which these few pages are based.

forms and is known by different names. The Genesis account, which tells how God divides the primeval ocean (Hebrew, *tehom*) into two parts, "the upper waters" and "the lower waters," recalls the "cleaving asunder" in the Babylonian account of Tiamat, the goddess of the deep from whose cleft body the upper and lower waters were formed.

Elsewhere in the Old Testament the reference is even more explicit. There the sea monster, representing the powers of chaos, is identified as the dragon (Job 7:12; Ps 74:13; Isa 51:9; Ezek 29:3, 32:2), Leviathan (Job 40:15–24; Ps 74:14, 104:26; Isa 27:1), Rahab (Job 9:13, 26:12; Ps 89:10; Isa 30:7, 51:9), and the serpent (Job 26:13: Isa 27:1; Amos 9:3). One of the clearest references is in Psalm 74:13, where the primeval ocean, the very epitome of disorder and chaos, is represented by a named sea monster with which the Creator is locked in deadly combat:

> By your power you cleft the sea monster in two
> and broke the sea serpent's heads in the waters;
> you crushed the head of Leviathan
> and threw him to the sharks for food
> (REB; cf. Job 26:12–13; Ps 89:9–11).

In other passages the imagery is adapted to refer, not to the act of God in creation, but to the activity of God in history and his intervention on behalf of his people Israel. Thus, in Isaiah 51:9–11 it is used to highlight God's deliverance of them from exile just as he had delivered them from Egypt (depicted here as elsewhere in scripture by the name "Rahab," cf. Isa 30:7; Ps 87:4):

> Was it not you who hacked Rahab in pieces
> and ran the dragon through?
> Was it not you who dried up the sea,
> the waters of the great abyss
> and made the ocean depths a path for the redeemed?
> The Lord's people, set free, will come back
> and enter Zion with shouts of triumph (REB).

But the adaptation is taken further still and applied, not only to the act of creation and not only to God's activity in history, but also to the time of the end when the redemption of his people would be complete. Thus, we read in the "little apocalypse" in Isaiah 24–27:

> On that day the Lord with his cruel sword,
> his mighty and powerful sword, will punish
> Leviathan that twisting sea serpent,
> that writhing serpent Leviathan;
> he will slay the monster of the deep (Isa 27:1 REB).

THE "FOUR GREAT BEASTS" IN DANIEL 7

The apocalyptic writers, not least the writer of Daniel, make good use of this same motif and describe in graphic language, culled from the Old Testament and from ancient tradition, the conflict between God the creator and the primeval forces of chaos.

The most graphic of these accounts is contained in Daniel 7 where Daniel, in a vision, sees "a great sea churned up by the four winds of heaven, and four great beasts rising out of the sea each one different from the others" (7:2–3 REB). The first beast is "like a lion and it had an eagle's wings"; the second is "like a bear"; the third is "like a leopard with four wings and four heads"; the fourth is "grisly and exceedingly strong," with great iron teeth and ten horns from which emerge "a little horn" with "eyes like human eyes and a mouth that uttered bombast" (7:4–9 REB). The influence of Hosea 13:7–8 can perhaps be detected at this point where a lion, a bear, and a leopard are mentioned together; but so too can that of the ancient combat myth.

Here in Daniel 7 it is adapted and applied to certain identifiable kings and kingdoms culminating in the tyrant Antiochus IV Epiphanes represented by "a little horn" on the head of the fourth beast.

But the reference contains greater depths than this. It has to do not just with political events and the fate of particular kings and kingdoms, but also with those cosmic forces of chaos and anarchy which they themselves exemplify and perpetuate. The picture here presented is that of a turbulent world, seething and boiling, producing from its depths all kinds of monsters at enmity with God. They rise out of the sea with great show of power and with bombastic pride in their own achievements. But they will come under the judgment of God; their end is at hand; they will be summarily and utterly destroyed. The language of the ancient myth expresses what cold prose could never do; what we have here is more than a purely "factual" description of the rise and fall of certain kings and kingdoms; it is a description of chaotic and evil powers, beyond the scope of the human will and the incidents of history, with which God the creator is in conflict and which at the end, in God's good time, will be subdued and slain.

BEHEMOTH AND LEVIATHAN

Elsewhere, in other apocalyptic writings, those fearsome beasts reappear with historical or eschatological reference. In the Psalms of Solomon 2:29 "the pride of the dragon" is a fairly obvious reference to the Roman general Pompey, and in the Damascus Document (from Qumran) the nations which oppose Israel are called "the serpent" (CD 8.10).

In certain other passages graphic reference is made to two mythical monsters called Behemoth and Leviathan (cf. 1 Enoch 60:7–9; 4 Ezra 6:49–52; 2 Bar. 29:4), reminiscent of the description given of the same two creatures in the book of Job (cf. 40:15–24, 41:1–34). In the 1 Enoch passage they appear in an eschatological context:

> On that day were two monsters parted, a female monster named Leviathan, to dwell in the abysses of the ocean over the fountains of the waters. But the male is named Behemoth, who occupied with his breast a waste wilderness. . . . And I besought the other angel

that he should show me the might of those monsters, how they were parted on one day and cast, the one into the abysses of the sea, and the other into the dry land of the wilderness (60:7–9).

It would appear that originally both those creatures were viewed as sea monsters; Leviathan, a female monster, retains this identity, but Behemoth, a male monster, is made to inhabit the land.

According to 4 Ezra 6 both these creatures came into being on the fifth day of creation and came to be separated in the following manner:

In the fifth day . . . you set apart two creatures; to one you gave the name Behemoth and to the other Leviathan. You put them in separate places, for the seventh part where the water was collected was not large enough to hold them both. You assigned to Behemoth as his territory a part of the land which was made dry on the third day, a country of a thousand hills; to Leviathan you gave the seventh part, the water. You have kept them to be food for whom you will and when you will (6:47–52).

Somewhat the same account is given in 2 Baruch where the eschatological setting is clearly set forth: "It will come to pass . . . that the Messiah will then begin to be revealed. And Behemoth will be revealed from his place, and Leviathan will ascend from the sea, those two great monsters which I created on the fifth day of creation, and I kept them until that time; and then they will be for food for all that are left" (29:3–4).

In this last reference we have a conflation of two mythical allusions: an eschatological banquet (cf. 25:6) and a great sea monster which is dragged ashore and devoured as food (cf. Ezek 38:4). The idea of an eschatological or "messianic" banquet was fairly widespread and is to be found in the Qumran texts and rabbinic sources as well as in the New Testament (cf. Luke 13:28–29; 22:30ff.; Rev 19:9). According to 2 Baruch, as we have seen, the two mythical monsters will be consumed as food for all the righteous who remain.

THE DRAGON IN REVELATION

In the book of Revelation the identification of the beast is of another kind: "Michael and his angels fought against the dragon. . . . The great dragon was thrown down, that ancient serpent, who led the whole world astray, whose name is the Devil, or Satan" (12:7–9 REB, cf. 20:2). Other beasts, which display the same devilish powers, meet the same fate as "the dragon" himself and are destroyed by the Messiah who appears in the form of a Lamb : "Then I saw the beast rise out of the sea; it had ten horns and seven heads. . . . The dragon conferred on it his own power. . . . The whole world went after the beast" (12:1ff. REB). Another beast comes up, this time out of the earth, which "spoke like a dragon and assumed all the authority of the first beast" (13:11ff. REB). The victory of "the Lamb" is proclaimed; the beasts and their devotees are made to drink "the cup of God's wrath" (14:1ff.).

The old creation myth, then, with its eternal conflict between God and the powers of chaos, is used as a vivid demonstration of God's activity on the side of the righteous and the pledge of his ultimate victory when chaos will be transformed into order and evil will be changed into good. Its precise meaning is not always clear, but it bears a powerful witness to the belief that, despite all appearances to the contrary, God is in control of history and will in the end bring all things to their successful and rightful conclusion.

THE COSMOS MYTH

Alongside the monster myth is another—what we might call the cosmos myth with which it is closely related in its use of symbolism and mythological imagery.

A DIFFERENT WORLD VIEW

We have just seen how, in the Old Testament and in the apocalyptic books generally, the old "conflict myth," with its fearsome mythological monsters, is used to depict the powers of chaos and so the powers of evil which find expression in kings and kingdoms and in cosmic forces that challenge not only Israel but the very authority of God.

Such a notion is closely linked in the apocalyptic books with a widespread belief in demons and Satan(s) and their "fall from grace" as a result of their illicit union with humankind (cf. Gen 6:1–4; 1 Enoch 6) or their rebellion in heaven against "the Lord of spirits" (cf. Jub. 4:15). The picture here presented is that of a great company of "fallen angels," sometimes identified as "stars," under the leadership of their demonic "prince," drawn up in battle array against the angelic hosts of heaven. Satan and his legions are in control of this present age; but "their doom is writ." In the new age to come the righteous and their angelic protectors will be vindicated and share in the ultimate triumph of God.

Besides this, as we have observed, is the mythological notion which sees earthly events in terms of their heavenly counterparts. The struggle here on earth between good and evil is to be understood in terms of a cosmic struggle in the heavenly realms between the powers of light and the powers of darkness. This is well illustrated once more in the book of Daniel (ch. 10) where the "princes," or guardian angels, of Greece and Persia confront Gabriel, Israel's intercessor and aide to Michael, Israel's "prince." The battles fought by the cosmic powers above determine the outcome of the battles fought by their human counterparts below.

This close relation between heaven and earth is again spelled out in mythological terms in the descriptions given of the visionary journeys made by Enoch and others to the ends of the earth and to heaven itself (cf. 1 Enoch 1–36;

37–71; T. Abr. etc.) where we are presented with what M. E. Stone calls "a mythological map of the world . . . closely related to Mesopotamian geographic conceptions."[3]

Such references as these indicate clearly an apocalyptic world view altogether different from our own, spelled out in mythological terms, which sees the eternal beyond the temporal, the unseen beyond the seen, a heavenly realm beyond the world of time and sense. It demonstrates a dualism that is both spatial (this present world over against the heavenly) and temporal (this historical scene over against the transcendent). It testifies also to the corruption of the cosmos and the part played in this by cosmic demonic powers; it recognizes that salvation cannot come from human endeavor or from "the historical process," but only from "outside" and that, in the end, evil will be destroyed, and God's kingdom will be established.

DEMYTHOLOGIZING WITHIN THE APOCALYPTIC BOOKS

It is of interest to observe that, even within the apocalyptic tradition itself, something like a "demythologizing" process had already begun. Alongside the cosmic dualism of "principalities and powers," for example, there was recognized an ethical dualism, to which reference has been made above, spelled out in terms of Adam's sin (cf. 2 Bar. 54:15, 19; 4 Ezra 3:21, etc.) into which all humankind had entered or in terms of the good and evil "inclinations" (cf. T. Asher 1:6, 8 etc.) for which men and women were themselves to be held ultimately responsible.

This is well illustrated in the Qumran scrolls and in a number of the apocalyptic books where reference is made to "the spirit of truth" and "the spirit of error" lodged in

---

[3]M. E. Stone, "Enoch and Apocalyptic Origins" in *Visionaries and the Apocalypses* (ed. P. D. Hanson; London: SPCK and Philadelphia: Fortress, 1983) 94.

the human heart. Sometimes these are personalized and correspond to the archangel Michael ("the angel of light") and to Satan or Beliar ("the angel of darkness"); at other times they correspond simply to the good and evil inclinations in human nature.

The apostle Paul expressed himself in somewhat the same way (cf. Rom 7:15ff.). He "took seriously the demonic nature of evil; but he no longer thought of 'principalities and powers' in terms of archons who govern the planets and the stars, but rather as the sum of all those forces in the universe that are opposed to Christ and his church."[4]

MYTH AND RESURRECTION

Further reference may be made at this point to another area of apocalyptic belief where a most significant breakthrough took place—the notion of resurrection from the dead. Belief in resurrection had, of course, been a familiar one in other cultures for many generations where, for example, the "death" of nature in the winter and its revival in the spring was depicted in the death and resurrection of the god. The identity of the god or his consort might vary from one culture to another, but the basic pattern remained the same and was expressed in similar mythological terms.

The apocalyptists' notion, however, was altogether different. Their belief in God's justice and coming deliverance pointed unerringly to a life beyond death which broke through all prevailing mythological concepts and declared in terms of resurrection the actual participation of the righteous in the life of heaven itself. Many of the trappings of mythological language remained—lakes of fire, unquenchable flames, a Great Trial, delights of paradise, and so on; but these cannot conceal the supreme significance of the

---

[4]Russell, *Divine Disclosure*, 136.

breakthrough that took place in religious thought at this
time, expressed most clearly for the first time in Daniel 12
and pursued in subsequent apocalyptic writings. Mythological representation gives way to actual participation in
the life of the world to come.

MYTH AND MEANING

What, then, are we to make of such literature, representing as it does a world view so different from our
own, written in symbolic language whose meaning so often
eludes us, and using mythological imagery that is frequently bizarre and grotesque? Were the rabbis right in
rejecting it as dangerous to Judaism, and was the early
church right in expressing hesitation over the acceptance
of the book of Revelation into the canon of scripture? What
worth has it for us in this modern age in giving us a clearer
understanding of the Christian gospel?

THE NEED TO "DEMYTHOLOGIZE"

Our assessment of that worth will be determined in
large measure by the interpretation we give to it, mythological language and all. In our attempt to understand its
meaning and its "relevance" for our day we may well wish
to "demythologize" its language and imagery and express
what it is saying in terms of our modern culture which our
contemporaries can understand. Some such exercise is indeed necessary if we are to make sense of its symbolism
within the setting of modern civilization. And yet, having
said that, it has to be confessed that such a process of
interpretation, by its very nature, carries with it no small
risk in the sense that the interpretation now given in the
"modern idiom" may be quite inadequate for the task in

hand, failing to catch all the nuances of the original and to convey its true meaning.

MYTHOLOGY MUST BE TAKEN SERIOUSLY BUT NOT LITERALLY

In any attempt at such demythologizing, not least our attempt to interpret the imagery of the apocalyptic writings, some wise words of Reinhold Niebuhr are worth bearing in mind: mythology, he comments, must always be taken "seriously, but not literally."[5]

First, it must be taken seriously. This means, among other things, that we are to pay proper respect to the text in question and to its mythological method of presentation. There is a temptation to cut off such a text from its mythological moorings, as from its historical moorings, and to allow its interpretation to drift into dangerous waters. One danger is to imagine that because it belongs to antiquity it must be antiquated and so out-of-date and irrelevant, with nothing to say to the modern mind. Another is to imagine that what is new must be true and that the modern form of interpretation must for this very reason be superior to the old. It may indeed be more understandable and more expressive of the prevailing culture, but it may in the process have lost something of its power and meaning and be less expressive of the truth contained in the very revelation it seeks to impart.

The modern reader must be humble enough to take seriously, then, what the monster myth and the cosmic myth are saying and not simply dismiss them as something otiose and irrelevant. John H. Yoder does well to remind us that "there is not and has never been within Christianity a single . . . universally self-evident rational base-line cos-

---

[5]R. Niebuhr, "The Truth in Myths," in *The Nature of Religious Experience* (ed. E. G. Bewkes; New York; n.p., 1937).

mology in contrast with which apocalyptic thought consti-
tutes a departure. . . . We do better not to ask a priori how
to play off an apocalyptic cosmology as a whole against
'reality' . . . [or to] investigate in what setting the apocalyptic vision of things, or specific statements within it, would
make sense."[6] Somewhat the same warning is given also by
Hans Küng to the reader faced with strange modes of
expression which do not fit in with his or her own world view
or preconceived understanding. He warns against allowing
stirred feelings, "to be replaced by intellectual comprehension,
images by concepts, stories by abstract ideas" and concludes
with the observation that *when the mythical element is
simply eliminated*—as became evident in the theology of
the Enlightenment and of liberalism—it is at the expense
of the Christian message which is thrown out together with
the myth. Faith then hardens into a rational religion."[7]

But, secondly, though myth must be taken seriously,
says Niebuhr, it must not be taken literally. The mode of
expression is not to be confused with the message it con-
veys; its meaning and "validity" are not bound inseparably
to its mythological expression. The literalist interpretation
not only refuses to see the revelation apart from its mode
of presentation, it at the same time evades the responsibility of trying to understand that revelation in terms of
today's culture and can all too easily end up in obscuran-
tism or in superstition. For its message to be recognized
and understood, it has to find expression in a language and
thought form to which men and women of today can
readily respond.

At the same time we must be honest enough to acknowledge that any act of "demythologizing" gives no guarantee that we have arrived at the heart of the message itself.

---

[6]John H. Yoder, "Armaments and Eschatology," *Studies in Christian Ethics* (n.d.) 51.
[7]Hans Küng, *On Being a Christian* (London: Collins, 1977) 414.

To demythologize in such a way is, in a sense, to remythologize, substituting for those of a bygone age the symbols and thought forms of our own generation and culture. It may be legitimate for preachers, for example, to follow up Paul's attempt to demythologize the "principalities and powers" by expressing them in terms of, say, political forces or social pressures or moral factors. Such an attempt to demythologize is both understandable and helpful—so long as we realize that we have in a way created a new or substitute mythology which in turn may also require in course of time to be demythologized and remythologized itself.

A FORM OF ESCAPISM?

There can be little doubt that this "change of focus" on the part of the apocalyptic writers—from the natural to the supernatural, from the mundane to the supramundane, from the historical to the transcendent, from "this present age" to "the age to come," from the rule of oppressors to the rule of God—was deeply influenced by the times in which they lived. We have seen that the books they produced represented "a protest literature," "a resistance literature," whether in terms of political tyranny or in terms of "the evil world" around. Thus in the book of Daniel, for example, we hear the desperate cry of the oppressed against the oppressor, a poignant appeal by the powerless against the powerful. It is a plea on the part of the author with which the reader can readily identify, whether in the second century B.C. or in any subsequent generation. It is not surprising that, in circumstances such as these, eyes have been raised to heaven, to the tranquillity and joys of another world where grief and pain, torture and death, are no more. So it was with the author of Daniel and his readers; and so also it has been down through the centuries in the religious traditions of Judaism, Islam, and Christianity alike.

THE DANGER OF ESCAPISM

But there is, of course, a danger that literature of this kind can easily lend itself to a form of escapism in which the readers are caught up into an imaginary world of fantasy and make-believe in which all wrongs are righted, the wicked are punished and the righteous justified. In the horizontal/historical apocalypses like that of Daniel, for example, they finds themselves in a supernatural world inhabited by legions of angels who, with super confidence, give complete assurance that the war in heaven has already been won, even though the corresponding battle on earth is still being grimly fought; and in the vertical apocalypses like 1 Enoch or the Testament of Abraham they accompany the seer to "the ends of the earth" and into heaven itself where they see ample evidence that "all will be well."

But although they might be tempted to remain for a while on some "cloud nine," far above the welter of earthly events, they, like the writer of the book, soon "come down to earth again" to face "life in the raw" with all its oppression and challenge. What they have seen in that supernatural world surpasses everything they have known in the natural world and prepares them to face all the trials that lie ahead. They come back, as it were, new people because, like the seer before them, they have seen things that the oppressor cannot see; they have experienced a world that the natural world around them cannot know. It has been for them, not some negative form of escapism, but a positive experience of divine assurance leading to moral resolve: their protests have been replaced by the promises of God, and their anguish has given way to affirmation that

God rules in human affairs. By the help of such books the readers could now see their present plight in the light of "the end," time in the light of eternity, the natural world in the light of the supernatural, "this age" in the light of "the age to come." This was no mere "whistling in the dark to keep their spirits up." It was a confidence born of conviction and leading to fuller commitment. They might be gripped firmly in the jaws of the beast; but even from that dubious vantage point they were able to see the gates of heaven and the glorious throne of God who ruled over all the earth and who would, when the time came, give his people the victory.

This is the picture vividly portrayed also in the book of Revelation: there John looks forward excitedly to the coming of Christ and the establishment of his eternal kingdom; but at the same time he can speak about it with complete confidence as if it were already here because of what he has seen and heard by revelation from above: "O Lord God, sovereign over all, you are and you were; we give you thanks because you have assumed full power and entered upon your reign" (Rev 11:17 REB). The vision of what will be confirms his faith and strengthens his resolve.

And this is the effect which this biblical apocalypse has had on countless generations of believers ever since. Some, no doubt, have found in it, as in the prophetic and apocalyptic literature generally, a means of escape from the drudgery and dangers of this life and have "taken off" in flights of fancy into some "never-never land." But to many others it has been a source of great encouragement and strength in facing the hard realities of life as they have come to know them. During dark days of persecution the books of Daniel and Revelation were read avidly and became a powerful incentive, not to relinquish life and give way to fantasy and daydreams, but to perseverance and faithfulness even to the point of torture and death.

THE DANGER OF FANATICISM

But if there is a danger of escapism and withdrawal from the world, there is also a danger of a quite different kind. It is the danger of fanaticism which sees a glorious future preordained and predetermined by God which embraces their own suffering, death, and even martyrdom in achieving its goal. It is possible that this was one of the reasons why, from quite an early date, the rabbis were extremely suspicious of such literature and came to condemn it so strongly. It is indeed a revolutionary literature which condemns wickedness and oppression of every kind and is not afraid to criticize those in power who wield undue authority over others. It is easy to see how some rulers could regard it as subversive and some religious leaders as dangerous. And so it has been regarded at many points in Jewish and Christian history, sometimes it must be said with a fair measure of justification. Where faith and fanaticism meet there is often a violent explosion, and these apocalyptic books have provided both ingredients. It is a danger which still exists and has a potential for harm as well as for good.

But the abuses to which such literature has lent itself should not blind us to the beneficial influence it has had and continues to have, not least in the history and witness of the Christian church. It is at the same time a protest against evil of every kind and a protestation that "the Lord God rules in human affairs," an expression of profound faith that God is to be trusted and will give to the faithful their just reward.

3

PREDICTION AND PROGNOSTICATION

APOCALYPTIC AND UNFULFILLED PROPHECY

It has been argued in chapter 1 that apocalyptic has a particular interest in unfulfilled prophecy whose meaning and significance it seeks to portray and whose true fulfillment it professes to disclose. Such prophecies had been made by divine inspiration and so carried with them a distinct authority which subsequent events could not negate. The prophet's word came as from the mouth of God himself and carried with it its own penetrating power. It could not and it would not fall helplessly to the ground, but must reach its target as foreordained by God. Prophecy, to be true prophecy, must be seen to be fulfilled.

But herein lay a great dilemma: the prophetic prediction could not fail because it was from God, and yet the prophetic writings seemed to be full of predictions and

promises whose "sell-by-date tag" had long since expired—
promises of a bright future for Israel, the judgment of its
enemies and the establishment of the universal rule of God.
Must the faithful Jew be impaled for ever on the horns of
such a dilemma? The apocalyptic writers gave to this question a resounding No!

Jeremiah's prophecy of the seventy years' captivity, as
we have already observed, was a case in point. Such a
prediction must stand firm, for it had divine authority for
its claim. Could it be that its true interpretation was other
than what it appeared to be? The seventy years' captivity,
says the writer of Daniel, was in fact a code for seventy
weeks of years. Here was the true interpretation of which
Jeremiah himself had been quite unaware! He spoke as the
oracle of God but in so doing did not realize the depth of
its meaning. In this way the old prophecy, instead of being
discredited, was revitalized and became a powerful word
from God, about to be fulfilled. Its hitherto hidden meaning had at last been disclosed.

We are reminded of the same kind of approach to
unfulfilled prophecy among the Qumran Community in, for
example, the so-called Habakkuk Commentary where it is
assumed that the prophet did not know the true meaning of
his own words. When interpreted by the Teacher of Righteousness it became clear that they referred, not to Habakkuk's day
at all, but to the life and times of the Qumran Community
itself. So it was with Jeremiah's prophecy: its true meaning,
as made known by Daniel, was now being revealed for the
very first time. The day of deliverance was at hand.

But when exactly would that great day dawn? Here
the author is quite specific: judgment would fall and
deliverance would come after an interval of three and
one half years ("time, two times and half a time," cf.
7:25, 9:27, 12:7). And so the readers waited; the foretold
time came—and passed! And still the prophecy remained
unfulfilled! The difficulty this caused may be surmised

from a reading of the book of Daniel itself where a re-adjustment of the precise date seems to be attempted in chapter 12, either by the author himself or by an editor. There the interval of three and one half years is lengthened to 3 years and 7 months (1,290 days, cf. 12:11) and then to 3 years and 8½ months (1,335 days, cf. 12:12).

Another illustration of such "readjustment" is to be found in the interpretation given at a later date to the fourth beast in Daniel 7. It is generally recognized (by nonconservative scholars at any rate) that the reference here is to the Greek or Hellenistic Empire which in course of time found expression in the person of Antiochus IV Epiphanes, represented here by "the little horn" of the beast. With the destruction of this beast God's kingdom would come. Once more the time came and went, with no obvious sign of fulfillment. Was the true interpretation, then, other than what had been assumed? The answer given by the writer of 4 Ezra around the year A.D. 100 was clear and unequivocal in its so-called eagle vision: "the eagle you saw rising out of the sea represents the fourth kingdom in the vision seen by your brother Daniel. But he was not given the interpretation which I am now giving" (12:11f.). The interpretation that follows points unerringly to the Roman Empire whose fall would usher in "the end." No doubt, as already noted, it was this identification of the fourth beast with Rome that helped the book of Daniel gain acceptance within the canon of scripture, not as a "failed apocalypse" but as an "about-to-be-fulfilled apocalypse" with a relevance that was powerful and indeed revolutionary in its divine revelation. This same identification with the Roman Empire is reflected in the Gospels and in the book of Revelation as well as in the early church fathers and is per-petuated within Christendom in the centuries that followed.

Such a process of interpretation and readjustment of prophecy, as we shall see more fully later, has continued right down to this present time, not only identifying the fourth beast with some modern expression of the Roman Empire, but also seeing the fulfillment of other prophecies and predictions in terms of present-day nations and states and of specified momentous events of our own time.

Given this method of interpretation, once the cord has been cut which tethers the prediction to a particular point in history, there is no end to the number of readjustments that become possible, and indeed are deemed necessary if the prophecy and the book in question are to retain their veracity and authority. Such readjustments are justifiable and proper, if used to indicate the principle that God's judgment falls inevitably on evil, whatever its form and whatever the generation responsible for it. But that is quite different from saying that all previous interpretations have been mistaken and that the interpretation now being given is the true and only one that can be trusted.

This form of interpretation assumes particularly graphic and, as we shall see, at times dangerous expression in the writings, sermons, and broadcasts of some present-day literalists who see in the prophecies and predictions of scripture an accurate forecast of the frightening events of our own day and a clear "proof" that "the end is nigh."

Such a process of interpretation has lent itself to much speculation and has been influenced by many factors. Among these has been the growth of what has come to be known as "dispensationalism" to which brief reference may now be made.

DISPENSATIONS AND DISPENSATIONALISM

IN THE APOCALYPTIC BOOKS

It will be recalled that one of the marks of the "historical" apocalyptic writings is the division of world history into great epochs, predetermined by God and systematically arranged in such a way that it was possible to identify at what points in the process the various historical events took place and how near to the end of history the readers themselves stood (see p. 23). The "millennia" or "dispensations" into which history was thus divided varied in length, but for the most part the schematization followed fairly well-defined patterns familiar to the world of that time.

Thus the author of Daniel, as we have seen, divides history from the exile onwards into seventy "weeks of years" which in turn are divided into three distinct epochs of seven "weeks," sixty-two "weeks" and one "week." In 1 Enoch 83–90 the same span of Israel's history is said to be ruled over by seventy "shepherds" whose reigns are divided into four periods ruled over by 12, 23, 23, and 12 "shepherds." This division of history into four is to be found also in Daniel in the four great beasts that rise out of the sea (Dan 7) and in the account of the great statue with its four metals (Dan 2). We may note that the Greek poet Hesiod used the same four metals to describe the idea of the four ages in a degenerating scale of values.

Somewhat similar schematization appears in the book of Jubilees and in the Assumption of Moses, based on the Old Testament notion of the "jubilee"; in the former the "jubilee" is reckoned as forty-nine years and in the latter fifty years; in both it is used as a measure of history to demonstrate, not only that it is divided into well-defined and recognizable periods or "Acts," but also that the curtain is about to rise on the dramatic final Act! The writers and their readers are able to identify these great historical epochs and know exactly where they themselves now stand in the course of history. They can see that everything so far has been fulfilled as planned by God and so they are encouraged to trust him to bring the whole of history to its glorious conclusion in the coming of his kingdom. This is brought out, for example, in the Apocalypse of Weeks contained in 1 Enoch 93:1–10 and 91:12–17 where history is divided into ten "weeks" of unequal lengths, seven of which have already passed; the three which are still to come refer to the messianic age at the close of which the final judgment will take place.

IN THE EARLY CHURCH

We shall look presently at the testimony borne in this connection by John in the book of Revelation and in particular at what he says concerning the coming of a millennial kingdom. Here we observe that, in course of time, the conception of divine "dispensations" came to feature quite prominently in the thinking of the early church and continued in different forms throughout the centuries that followed. It was a notion that lent itself to much speculation, not least in trying to ascertain the time of the parousia of Christ. Thus, as early as the time of Irenaeus (ca. 130–200) it is stated that, just as in the beginning God created the world in six days before resting on the Sabbath day, so he had ordained that that same world would continue for six epoch-"days" of one thousand years each before its consummation when the "Sabbath rest" of his appointing would be ushered in.[1] The antichrist would take control and reign for three and one-half years (cf. Dan 9:27), but the power and the kingdom would be taken from him and given to "the saints of the Most High" (Dan 7:27).

The general expectation was that the time of the consummation was close at hand. Thus, the Montanists, for example, gave a precise date for its coming and left their homes to await its arrival—an action that has been repeated by many groups on many occasions ever since. Irenaeus himself did not share their conviction concerning

---

[1]See John G. Gammie, "A Journey through Danielic Spaces," in *Interpreting the Prophets*, 261ff.

its precise date, though Tertullian (ca. 169–200) apparently did, basing his belief, as others also did, on the evidence of the book of Daniel.

An important development took place in the writings of Hippolytus (ca. 170–236), a disciple of Irenaeus, and his contemporary Africanus, who not only affirmed that the world would last for 6,000 years, but calculated that Jesus had been born in the year 5550 after creation, leaving 450–500 years to run before the consummation and his second advent. Here, then, we have in fact two developments of some moment: the projection of the hope of his coming from the immediate to the distant future and the giving of a precise date for "the end." The year 500, however, came and went with no great flurry of expectation. More dramatic was the period around the year 1000, marking the close of the thousand years of "Sabbath rest" when Christ would surely come.

IN SUBSEQUENT HISTORY

Ever since those early days history has been replete with illustrations of this kind of expectation and prediction, often based on a "dispensationalist" understanding of it. A particularly influential interpretation of this kind was introduced in the late twelfth century by Joachim of Fiore (1145–1202) who, by divine revelation, was shown that history was moving through three ascending ages, each presided over by the persons of the Trinity: the first was the age of the Father (or the Law), the second the age of the Son (or the Gospel), and the third the age of the Spirit whose coming would be like the dawn over against the darkness—the "Sabbath rest" for all humankind when love, joy, and freedom would reign supreme.[2]

---

[2]See Norman Cohn, *The Pursuit of the Millennium: Revolutionary Millenarians and Mystical Anarchists of the Middle Ages* (rev. and exp. ed.; New York: Oxford University Press, 1970) 108f.

When viewed in the light of the prophetic scriptures, and not least the book of Revelation, this interpretation, like that of others before it, not only detected a distinct pattern within history, it also made possible the forecasting of its future course. It was an interpretation that remained in vogue throughout Europe for several centuries to come, albeit with variations and different emphases. Thus, in the early sixteenth century one Bernt Rothmann, an Anabaptist in Münster, taught a doctrine of "the Three Ages" in which the first was the age of sin culminating in the Flood; the second the age of persecution and the cross; the third (now about to begin) the age of vengeance and triumph for the saints. The time of trouble was at an end; Christ was coming in his second advent; to prepare for that coming he had set up his kingdom in the town of Münster.[3]

Norman Cohn, in his fascinating book *The Pursuit of the Millennium*, traces with ample illustration the effect of such a belief in predetermined "ages" or "dispensations" from the time of the early church right down to the rise of Marxism in the early years of the twentieth century. Such expectations lent themselves, as we have seen, to predictions concerning the time and place of the coming kingdom and the identification of messianic figures who would prepare the way for the second advent of Christ. Again and again precise forecasts were made concerning the breaking in of the kingdom on the evidence of scriptural prophecy. P. D. Hanson lists a number of these,[4] often based on numerological calculations: in 420 it was confidently announced that the end of the world would come between February 10 and 14 of that year; in 1666 a Jewish itinerant preacher caused great

---

[3]Ibid., 274.
[4]P. D. Hanson, *Old Testament Apocalyptic* (Interpreting Biblical Texts; Nashville: Abingdon, 1987) 47f.

commotion in Palestine by announcing that he was the promised Messiah; in 1844 a Christian group in the United States called the Millerites sold all their possessions and awaited the return of Christ. As recently as 1992 similar expectations were raised in Korea by the claims of a self-professed Messiah. And so on the illustrations could go. Interpretations of this kind point to identifiable "signs of the times" which purport to demonstrate that ancient prophecy concerning "the end" finds its fulfillment in named individuals or nations or in specific movements within history. As forecast dates indicating "the end" have come and passed by, readjustments have had to be made and new limits attached so that dashed hopes have become deferred hopes as successive adaptations have been made and new calculations substituted for old.

In More Recent Times

It is clear from a reading of church history that "dispensationalism" and "adventism" have gone hand in hand, perhaps never more so than among "fundamentalist" Christians in the nineteenth and twentieth centuries. The word "dispensationalism" has come to be used to describe a system of biblical interpretation, associated with the name of J. N. Darby (1800–1882), founder of the Plymouth Brethren.[5] It is an elaborate scheme "popularized" to help "students of the Bible" by C. I. Scofield (1843–1921) in the Scofield Reference Bible (1908, rev. ed. 1917 and 1966) which has served as a guide to fundamentalist belief ever since. It propounds a scheme by which the Bible, taken in its entirety, discloses God's grand design for humankind's

---

[5]See Alexander Reese, *The Approaching Advent of Christ: An Examination of the Teaching of J. N. Darby and his Followers* (London and Edinburgh: Marshall, Morgan and Scott, 1937).

salvation in a series of seven dispensations, each with its own "test." These range from the age of "innocence" (cf. Gen 1:28) to the coming of the "millennial kingdom" (cf. Rev 20) and the second advent of Christ. The sixth dispensation is now almost at an end, and the "Sabbath rest" of the millennial kingdom is to be expected at any moment when Christ will return to earth to establish his royal reign of one thousand years.

Expectations and prognostications relating to the second advent are perhaps most prevalent in times of world crisis or national tragedy, and so it has been throughout the past century or so with its two great world wars, the subsequent "Cold War" and the ever present threat of nuclear catastrophe. Even with the easing of world tension, the expectation, with its accompanying prognostications, is apparently no less marked and is held firmly by millions of Christians in Europe, the New World, and the Orient alike.

Such expectation, of course, is firmly embedded in the scriptural revelation that, as Christ came in his incarnation to establish his kingdom, so he will come again at the consummation to assume authority and to deliver the kingdom into the hands of God the Father. But we do well to note that concerning that day and that hour we know not. We recall in this connection the warning given by Jesus to his disciples which is as apposite today as it was then: "Lord, is this the time at which you are to restore sovereignty to Israel?" to which he replied, "It is not for you to know about dates and times which the Father has set within his own control" (Acts 1:6f. REB; Mark 13:32). It is a warning that has not always been sufficiently heeded in the church's search for "the mystery of the kingdom." Part of that "mystery," about which there has been much debate and much speculation through the centuries, has been the notion of the "millennial kingdom."

MILLENNIALISM AND
THE MILLENNIAL KINGDOM

IN REVELATION 20 AND RELATED WRITINGS

In Revelation 20:1–7 John gives a vivid picture of the founding of a "millennial kingdom" at the time of the parousia of Christ—the only occurrence of such a reference in the Bible. The text is not easy to interpret, but it seems to indicate that, with the appearance of Christ, such a kingdom will be set up on the earth and will last for one thousand years, participated in not only by those who are alive at that time but also by others who had been martyred for their faith and who would be resurrected to take part in it. Together they would reign with Christ their Lord. Throughout the duration of the kingdom, Satan would be bound in chains; at its close he would be released and would attack "the saints," but would be defeated and thrown into the lake of fire (20:1–10). A general resurrection and a final judgment would then ensue, to be followed by the renewal of heaven and earth (20:11–21:8) and the appearance of the new Jerusalem (21:9–22:20).

This hope in the coming of an "intermediary" kingdom, it would seem, was part of the prevailing apocalyptic expectation at that time which finds expression in other apocalyptic writings besides that of Revelation. In 4 Ezra, for example, dating from around the same period as the biblical apocalypse, it is said that God will establish on earth a kingdom which will last for four hundred years (cf. 7:28) at the close of which the Messiah and all the righteous who have taken part with him in it will die. After some days of "primeval silence" there will be a general resurrection for judgment and the dawning of "the age to come." A somewhat similar picture is given in 2 Enoch where, after a preliminary judgment, the Messiah will reign in his kingdom for one thousand years (cf. 32:3–33:2). Once more this kingdom will mark the end of "this present age" and will be followed by "a new creation" and "the age to come."

Behind this vision of a millennial kingdom there lay a lively hope, already expressed in the Old Testament, that God would indeed set up a kingdom here on earth in which his people would enjoy all kinds of material and spiritual blessings, a veritable Golden Age in which people and nature would participate. The picture given in the prophecy of Isaiah is typical:

> No child there will ever again die in infancy,
> No old man fail to live out his span of life;
> He who dies at a hundred is just a youth,
> And if he does not attain a hundred
> he is thought accursed (Isa 65:20f. REB).

It is a glorious age in which nature itself will share to the full. Here is how the writer of 2 Baruch sees it: "when the Messiah will begin to be revealed" (29:3), "the earth will yield fruits ten thousand-fold. And on one vine will be a thousand branches, and one branch will produce a thousand clusters, and one cluster will produce a thousand grapes, and one grape will produce a cor of wine" (2 Bar. 29:5).

But alongside this prophetic vision of a golden age, John no doubt had in mind another of a quite different kind: the vision recorded in Ezekiel 38–39 which tells how Israel will be attacked by the heathen nations led by a mysterious prince named Gog. John sees this vision being fulfilled within the context of the coming kingdom: Satan will be let loose and will seduce the nations of the earth; he will muster them for war; "the hosts of Gog and Magog" will besiege Jerusalem, but fire will come down from heaven and consume them; the seducer, the devil himself, will be thrown into the lake of fire (cf. 20:7–10).

DIFFICULT EXEGESIS

The whole passage presents us with a number of difficult exegetical problems, so much so that, in the words of A. T. Hanson, "millenarianism . . . is an element in the New Testament which modern critical theology has not attempted to incorporate and is therefore left to the adventists and literalists to expound."[6] It is certainly difficult to reconcile with what we find elsewhere in the New Testament, nor does it tie in readily with what we read elsewhere in Revelation itself. Hence the ongoing controversy and debate.

For a long time it was customary to give it a spiritual or allegorical interpretation or else to see in it a collage of traditional eschatological themes which were not always consistent or reconcilable. Or, it has been suggested, John's intention, in presenting this traditional picture of a glorious messianic age, may have been quite simply to press home some particular theological message. J. W. Mealy, for example, has argued that the millennium as presented here by John, is not in fact "a unique period in the life of the redeemed," but "an age of just recompense, expressed in the temporary denial of resurrection to the unrepentant."[7] In this case. John's words are to be seen as an encouragement to loyalty on the part of all Christians to the point of death in a time of persecution leading up to the parousia.

A CHECKERED HISTORY

The doctrine of a millennial kingdom has had a checkered history but, as John G. Gammie has suggested, "millennialism and dispensationalism have been a more

---

[6]A. T. Hanson, "Eschatology" in *A New Dictionary of Christian Theology* (ed. A. Richardson and J. Bowden; London: SCM, 1983) 186.

[7]J. W. Mealy, *After the Thousand Years: Resurrection and Judgment in Revelation 20* (JSNTSup 70; Sheffield: JSOT Press, 1992).

integral part of Christian thought down through the centuries than many of us have cared to acknowledge."[8] He gives ample illustration of this from the time of Irenaeus (ca. 130–200) onwards. It is indeed significant that from as early a time as this we find this doctrine being given such strong expression. On the basis of the books of Daniel and Revelation, and with the support of 2 Thessalonians, Irenaeus expresses his strongly held belief in a new era which will mark the consummation of world history as hitherto known and the introduction of a thousand years' reign on earth of Christ and his "saints." This belief persisted with different emphases right down to the time of the Protestant Reformation and was expounded in different ways by both Luther and Calvin. In the preface to his *Commentary on Daniel,* published in 1537, Luther professed his belief that the end of the world was close at hand. Calvin was less certain about the immediacy of the kingdom but did not doubt that it would at last arrive. For a time following the Reformation, the belief was maintained by the Anabaptists among others and is perpetuated today for the most part by Adventists and other conservative evangelical bodies, albeit with diverse interpretations attached.

DIVERSE INTERPRETATIONS

From what has been said above, it might be assumed that, among those who accept the "millennialist" position, there is basic agreement concerning the circumstances surrounding the expected second advent of Christ. This, however, is very far from being the case. Millennialism in fact comes in many shapes and sizes, and diverse interpretations are given of the millennial concept itself and of many elements within it. It would be presumptuous to claim to explain in a few brief lines what is a highly complex subject,

---

[8]John G. Gammie, "Journey," 271.

and the reader is referred to a book like *The Meaning of the Millennium,* edited by Robert G. Clouse,[9] in which four interpretations are given by four contributors representing diverse millennial views. The editor himself, in the introduction (to which I am indebted), attempts brief definitions or descriptions of three main lines of approach, the first of which shows within itself a diversity of interpretation. These are: premillennialism (historic premillennialism and dispensational premillennialism), postmillennialism, and amillennialism. These very designations can, however, be misleading, for differences of judgment are expressed not just concerning the expected time of the second advent and the establishment of the millennial kingdom, as these designations might suggest, but also concerning the very nature of that coming and that kingdom and the part to be played in it by Christ and his saints.

In the premillennialist understanding, there will be certain recognizable signs preceding the return of Christ among which are the preaching of the gospel to all nations, a great apostasy, wars accompanied by natural catastrophes, the appearance of the antichrist (see below, pp. 80f.), and a great tribulation. Christ will reign, together with his saints, in a prolonged era of unprecedented peace and righteousness in which the ancient prophecies will be seen to be fulfilled when all creation will know and reflect the blessings of God. In this kingdom the Jews will be converted (there are marked differences of interpretation at this point concerning the "how" and the "when" of such conversion) and will play an important part in it.

There is division of opinion too concerning the nature of the participation of the saints in the millennial kingdom—whether in their physical or in their spiritual bodies. The literalist interpretation accepts that they will rise in

---

[9]*The Meaning of the Millennium: Four Views* (ed. Robert J. Clouse; Downers Grove, Ill.: InterVarsity, 1977).

their physical bodies to share with those still alive during the reign of Christ on earth. At the close of the millennium there will be a resurrection of the rest of the dead, who will then experience for eternity the states of either heaven or hell. We may observe at this point that, according to dispensationalist teaching like that of J. N. Darby, there are to be two returns of Christ prior to the millennium: the first is a secret return for the "Rapture" of the church before the great tribulation when believers will be "caught up" to meet their Lord in the air (cf. 1 Cor 15:5) so that they will "always be with the Lord" (cf. 1 Thess 4:13–18). After a seven years' period of tribulation Christ will return to earth to establish his millennial kingdom.[10]

At the close of the millennium, Satan, who had been bound and imprisoned in a "bottomless pit" for one thousand years, is "let loose for a little while" (Rev 20:3 REB), during which time believers are sorely tried. But at the close of the thousand years he is thrown into "the lake of fire and brimstone" to suffer the fate of "the beast" and "the false prophet" through whom he had performed his will (cf. Rev 20:10). Then comes the end and the creation of the new heaven and the new earth in an unending era of heavenly bliss.

In the foregoing paragraphs concerning the premillennialist position little attempt has been made, for clarity's sake, to distinguish between historic premillennialism and dispensational premillennialism. According to G. E. Ladd two distinctive marks of the dispensational premillennialists are: (i) the clear distinction between Israel and the church, the salvation of the Jewish people, the rebuilding of the Jerusalem temple and the reinstatement of the sacrificial system in keeping with Ezekiel 40–48; and (ii) a literal

---

[10]Cf. J. E. Walvoord, *The Rapture Question* (Findlay, Ohio: Dunham, 1957), and *The Blessed Hope and the Tribulation* (Grand Rapids: Eerdmans, 1976).

system of biblical interpretation as distinct from a historical interpretation, particularly as this is applied to the Old Testament.[11] The historic premillennialists (i) also recognize the salvation of the Jews but see this in a different light in that they will be converted on the same basis as the Gentiles, through faith in Jesus Christ; and (ii) many Old Testament passages which applied in their historical setting to historical Israel have in the New Testament been applied to the church,[12] and so they refuse to form their eschatology by means of a literal interpretation of the Old Testament into which the New Testament is then fitted, but form their theology from the explicit teaching of the New Testament itself.

Reference to the postmillennial and amillennial lines of approach can be made much more briefly. According to the postmillennialist the kingdom is being extended throughout the world as the gospel is being taught and preached; the scope and influence of Christianity will be such that, in due course, there will come to the world a prolonged era of peace and prosperity. There will be no catastrophic break between the world as it has been and the coming of this "millennium," but rather a gradual growth as more and more people are converted. The incidence of evil, though still present, will decrease with the ever-increasing influence of Christianity, and many of the world's social and economic problems will be solved. Then Christ will appear in his second advent. The dead will be raised and the final judgment will take place.

According to the amillennialist, however, there will be no such era of peace as that envisaged by the postmillennialist and no gradual and inevitable triumph of good

---

[11] See G. E. Ladd, "Historic Premillennialism," in *Meaning of the Millennium*, 19.
[12] Ibid., 27.

over evil. God's kingdom is in fact already present here on earth; good and evil still strive for the mastery, with no obvious or dramatic conquest on either side. Christ is Lord and ruler of his kingdom which, with his second advent, will be established as a perfect kingdom within a new creation. The millennial kingdom to which Revelation 20 refers is not an earthly kingdom at all but refers to the state of those who have "died in Christ" and now reign with him in heaven.

Readers who have studied the scriptures through the eyes of historical criticism will no doubt be both bemused and puzzled by this whole approach to biblical interpretation and in particular by the degree of speculation involved (and often the amount of heat engendered!). But there can be no doubt that it has a large following, especially in its premillennialist form, among many conservative evangelical Christians the world over. It is a subject that cannot be brushed aside if only because, as we shall see more clearly later in this chapter, it has had such wide influence, particularly in the United States, not just on theological thinking but also on the interpretation of politics and world events in this present generation.

THE ANTICHRIST

Brief mention may be made at this point of the figure of the antichrist who, it was believed, would appear in "the last days" and do battle with God and his Messiah. The term first appeared in Christian writings, but its origins are to be traced back into the Old Testament and beyond. Of special significance in this regard is the reference in Ezekiel 38:2 to "Gog of the land of Magog" who would lead the forces of evil against God and his people. Behind this figure we may find traces of the old combat myth to which allusion has already been made.

In the Jewish apocalyptic writings, this antichrist—by whatever name—is often identified with some historical figure who had a reputation for evil deeds. It is not surprising to find Antiochus IV Epiphanes, for example, given this role or, in later years, the Emperor Nero. Sometimes, however, he is presented, not as a human figure at all, but as the embodiment of Beliar, the prince of demons. According to the Testament of the Twelve Patriarchs, for example, God's Messiah will wage war against him (cf. T. Dan 5:10); Beliar will be routed and "cast into the fire for ever" (T. Jud. 25:3). Elsewhere it is said that he will perform miraculous signs and will deceive many people, but God will destroy both him and those who put their trust in him (cf. Sib. Or. 3:63ff.). The same allusion is made in the book of Revelation where the dragon, who fights against Michael in heaven (cf. Rev 12:1–17) is none other than this demonic antichrist.

Throughout the course of world history, this demonic figure has been identified with one historical personage after another from Nero through Napoleon to Hitler! Despite these various and vain attempts at identification, the figure itself remains a potent symbol. In the words of H. H. Rowley, "Beneath the mistaken hopes we can see a sound instinct. . . . The demonic Beliar stands for a persistent force of evil, not in any one person alone, but behind all evil people, incarnate in them in varying degrees. The human antichrist stands, alas! for the recurring antichrists the world has seen. . . . Just as the lustful and the violent of one generation much resemble the lustful and the violent of another, so the antichrist of one generation resembles the antichrist of another, for he has the same spirit of Beliar in him."[13]

---

[13] H. H. Rowley, *The Relevance of Apocalyptic* (rev. ed.; Cambridge: Lutterworth, 1963) 174.

PREDICTION AND POLITICS

THE JUDGMENT OF THE GENTILES
AND THE SALVATION OF THE JEWS

In the apocalyptic writings increasing interest is taken in the destiny of the individual soul after death; but it remains true that their primary interest is nationalistic rather than individualistic. Their chief concern is with the judgment of the Gentiles and the salvation of Israel.[14] Sometimes the distinction made is ethical rather than ethnic; but the implication, if not the actual claim, is that on the one hand there are "the wicked Gentiles" and on the other "the righteous Israel."

As a result of this, it can be said with a fair measure of certainty that apocalyptic grew out of the soil of politics, whether of a religious or a secular kind. We have already seen that, for the most part, its background is that of persecution under Antiochus, disillusionment under the Hasmoneans, and harassment under the Romans. The protest was leveled, not just against a corrupt society, but also against oppressive governments, not least those that seemed to assume the rights and prerogatives of God himself. Rulers and nations come in for severe criticism and are the object of dire threats. Israel suffered greatly at the hands of such men, but in the end Israel will be saved and will be amply rewarded with the material as well as the spiritual blessings of God.

It is true that in the apocalyptic books, as in the prophetic books generally, there is an ambivalence on the part of these writers in their attitude towards the Gentiles. In some the hope is expressed that the day will come when

---

[14] For a fuller account see Russell, *Method and Message of Jewish Apocalyptic*, 297ff.

"coasts and islands will wait for (God) and look to (him) for protection" (Isa 51:5 REB), "the holy temple will be called God's house for all nations" (Isa 56:7), and his blessings will be shared, not only with "Israel, my inheritance," but also with "Egypt, my people" and "Assyria, the work of my hands" (Isa 19:25). The time will come when the Gentiles will acknowledge Israel and Israel's God, offering to him their adoration (cf. 1 Enoch 10:21) and come with Israel to share in the worship of the glorious temple (T. Benj. 9:2; 10:5, 9f.; cf. Rev 21:24ff.; 22:2).

But it remains true that, for the most part, the Gentiles continue to be regarded as the traditional enemies of Israel, meriting the judgment of God and facing his awful wrath (cf. Isa 63:1–6). They are the very incarnation of evil (cf. Zech 14:1ff.) whose doom is sealed (cf. Ezek 38–39). They will be destroyed in God's fury (cf. Isa 34:1ff.; Jer 25:29–38); the day of the Lord will be a day of vengeance (cf. Jer 46:10). The same theme is continued in the extrabiblical apocalyptic books. Those Gentiles who have repented of their evil ways will indeed be spared and given a servile place; but all the rest will be destroyed (cf. 2 Bar. 72:2–6). In the earlier apocalyptic books also we hear the same hard attitude being expressed: "All the peoples, nations and languages" will be made to serve "the saints of the Most High" (Dan 7:14) or else will be destroyed (cf. Dan 2:44, cf. 7:11f.).

The same attitude is adopted by the writers of 1 Enoch: the earth will swallow them up as it did Korah of old (90:18); the righteous will slay them with the sword (91:12); the Messiah will be the instrument of God's wrath and will "destroy the godless nations with the word of his mouth" (Pss. Sol. 17:17); and those who remain will be made to serve under Israel's yoke (cf. 1 Enoch 17:32ff.). This bitter hatred of the Gentiles is expressed even more clearly elsewhere: the Gentiles will be driven out of Palestine (cf. Jub. 23:30; 50:5); angels will be set over them, will lead them astray, and effect their destruction (cf. 1 Enoch 15:31); they will be consigned to the flames of Gehenna (cf. Ass. Mos. 10:10); even though they "bring gifts and presents and tokens of homage" (1 Enoch 53:1), these will be of no avail; they will be destroyed and banished from the face of the earth (cf. 1 Enoch 53:2). Gentile kings and rulers will be removed from their thrones; they will be filled with shame and "worms will be their bed" (1 Enoch 46:4–6); they will fall down in anguish, but their prayers for mercy will be of no avail; the righteous will rejoice to see their fearful plight (cf. 1 Enoch 62:1ff.).

So too in 4 Ezra. The law of God, given to the Jews, had been offered also to the Gentiles, but it was rejected by them. On the day of judgment they will be resurrected and condemned to eternal torment because they have despised his commandments; the pit of torment and hell is reserved for them (cf. 7:26). In the last days the multitude of the nations will be gathered together to make war against God's Messiah (cf. 13:5, 34; Ezek 38–39); the Messiah will fight against them with the help of supernatural powers and "a fiery stream" issuing from his mouth will utterly destroy them (cf. 13:10) so that only "dust of ashes and smell of smoke" remain (13:11).

Such bitterness and hatred are no doubt to be seen in the light of the dire persecution and deprivation that Israel had to face from the time of Antiochus to the fall of Jerusalem in A.D. 70 and beyond. But even when such extenuating circumstances are taken fully into account, the venom poured out on the Gentiles is indeed deadly and shows how far removed they were from the universalistic vision held by some of their prophetic forebears.

Corresponding to this theme of the judgment of the Gentiles, and as its corollary, is that of the salvation of Israel to whom would be given "the kingly power, sovereignty and greatness of all the kingdoms under heaven" (Dan 7:27 REB). Such blessings would be shared by all Israel; the "lost tribes" of the north, who had been taken captive by the

Assyrians, would be reunited with their compatriots to take part with them in the final triumph of God's own people (cf. Isa 11:12; Pss. Sol. 17:28; 4 Ezra 13:12, 39).

AN "ARMAGEDDON THEOLOGY"

The scenario thus presented is indeed a frightening one. But more frightening still—and more reprehensible—is the interpretation often given of such predictions by those who, in the name of Christ, anticipate with eager expectation the slaughter of "the nations" ("the wicked"), a slaughter from which God's own people "Israel" ("the true church," they themselves) would alone be saved.

The long history of the Christian church tells all too often the sad story of how men and women, in the name of the Prince of Peace and on the supposed authority of scripture, engaged in the most terrible slaughter of their enemies, be they "Jews, Turks, heretics, or whatsoever." A lethal concoction of revolutionary politics and religious fanaticism found explosive expression in militant millenarianism which put its trust not just in the power of God but also in the power of the sword to establish his kingdom here on earth. Among the best known illustrations of this is the story of Thomas Müntzer and his followers who by force sought to set up "the kingdom" in the town of Münster only to die by the sword. The "sword of justice" which was to extend the boundaries of the kingdom throughout the whole world was to wreak its own terrible vengeance in the massacre of that town's entire population.

The notion of a great conflict between the powers of good and the powers of evil as a prelude to the second advent of Christ has a long history behind it and claims to find its authority in certain Old and New Testament passages, prominent among which is Revelation 16:16 where reference is made to the battle of Armageddon, a site in northern Israel. Favorite supporting prophecies in the exposition of this passage are Ezekiel 38–39, Zechariah 13–14, and Revelation 14, which are usually conflated and used to interpret one another in terms of the fast approaching end. Together they build up a picture of that fearful day when God will do battle with the powers of evil on the earth and wreak his terrible vengeance upon them. He will defend his people, at whatever cost to the earth and to "the nations" who live on it. It is seen as no mere mythological conflict, but as a real battle in which literally millions of people will die. The slaughter will be such that the blood of the slain will reach even to the horses' bridles (cf. Rev 14:20). There will be "plundering, spoiling, and stripping" of villages and towns (cf. Ezek 38:12 REB), and many millions of people will be slain (cf. Zech 13:8f.).

The system of exposition and interpretation surrounding such a belief has come to be known as "Armageddon theology." This, in effect, declares that, before the second advent of the Son of man takes place, this battle to end all battles will be fought, at the time of the great tribulation, in which Christ will lead his armies to victory over the armies of Satan. It is openly claimed by many dispensationalists, for example, that it is now almost upon us and that we must, as nations and as individual believers, make preparation for its coming. There will be no peace on earth until the Prince of Peace himself appears, and so all talk of peace and all "pacts" for peace before that time are tantamount to a betrayal of our Lord. The battle must be fought and won.

The earth itself will be devastated and laid waste. This is made graphically clear by Hal Lindsey, for example, who gives to one of his books the title *The Late Great Planet Earth*, a title which speaks for itself.[15] The conflict envis-

---

[15] *The Late Great Planet Earth* (Grand Rapids: Zondervan, 1970). Among Hal Lindsey's other books are *There's a New World Coming* (Irvine, Calif.: Harvest House, 1973 and Coverdale House, 1974); *Satan*

aged, he suggests, is obviously that of a nuclear war. Prophecies of "fire, smoke and brimstone" are clearly references
to nuclear explosion, radioactive fall-out, and melted earth!
The locusts which appear as agents of God's wrath are
Cobra helicopters, their deadly sting is the nerve-gas
sprayed from the helicopters' tails! The "corpses" of "the
two witnesses" referred to in Revelation 11 are to be seen
by the people of "all languages and nations"—by satellite
television!

It is hardly conceivable that such beliefs as these can
be entertained today by professing Christians, but the fact
remains that this is so. It follows from such surmising that
disarmament, for example, is contrary to the will of God
and that preparation for nuclear war is a duty laid upon us
so that Armageddon may be fought and won, that Satan
and his legions may be defeated, and that Christ may come
in his second advent to establish his kingdom of peace
on earth!

But not only is the battle of Armageddon thus specified, the combatants in that battle are actually identified.
With a confidence and an assurance that outmatches that
of prophet and apocalyptist, the same interpreter is able to
identify, even by name, those nations and peoples in league
with Satan and so at enmity with God. In many such
pronouncements in recent years (at least until the breakup
of the Soviet Empire) "the enemy" has frequently been
identified as "world communism" which has been dubbed
"the Satan" or "the antichrist" and which must be defeated
and destroyed "that the scriptures might be fulfilled" and
that the kingdom might come on earth "with power." In
such circumstances, it is the duty of "a Christian nation"
(like that of the United States or Britain) to prepare by
all means, including that of nuclear build-up, for the

is Alive and Well on Planet Earth (Grand Rapids: Zondervan, 1972 and
London: Marshall, Morgan and Scott, 1973).

fight against this antichrist and not to shirk even "first strike" action.

But the identification of "the enemy" is more precise even than this. Here is a fairly typical statement said to have been made in 1982 by the influential TV evangelist Pat Robertson in the United States, paraphrasing the opening verses of Ezekiel 38: "In the latter days when Israel is regathered from the nations, I am going to cause something to happen. Here is what is going to happen. I am going to put hooks in the jaws of the confederation that is going to be led by someone named Gog in the land of Magog (the Soviet Union). And the people that will be with it are Beth Togarma (Armenia), Put (Libya), Rush (Ethiopia), Gomer (South Yemen) and Persia (Iran)."[16] Others have sought to confirm such prognostications by pointing out that the mythological Gog is described as "the prince of Rosh" and that two cities of Rosh are named as Meshech and Tubal, names which are "remarkably similar to Moscow and Tubolsk, two capital cities of Russia today"![17] Other writers have identified the Soviet Union, Red China, and the European Economic Community respectively as Gog (or "the people from the north" in Daniel 11:11 etc.), "the king of the east" in Revelation 16:12, and the "ten horns of the beast" in Daniel 7:7.[18] Given such a literalist approach, a poor sense of history, a limited conception of biblical revelation, a wildly speculative mind, and a vivid imagination, such a development, it may be said, is almost inevitable.

The illustrations given above are perhaps not altogether typical of the interpretations offered by many other literalists and dispensationalists, but they offer a solemn warning not to allow prophecy and prediction to lose their

[16] Grace Halsell, *Prophecy and Politics: Militant Evangelists on the Road to Nuclear War* (Westport, Conn.: Lawrence Hill and Co., 1986) 16.
[17] Ibid., 32.
[18] Ibid., 24.

grip on history or to surrender to a speculative faith which forgets the roots from which it has sprung and the historical context in which these roots were firmly embedded.

THE DESTINY OF ISRAEL

This interpretation of prophecy and apocalyptic, which envisages "the end" in terms of an Armageddon judgment on "the nations," has much to say also concerning the destiny of Israel and its salvation "in the last days." The fundamentalist/dispensationalist world view is as decidedly pro-Israel as it is anti–communist. Israel has a special place in the providence and plan of God and will in the end be "saved." The promises made to Israel concerning its occupation of the land of Palestine must be fulfilled, and so its claim over territory that has lain in other hands for centuries is fully justified. For this reason, the Six Days War of 1967 was an outstanding landmark, for it restored to Israel the kingdom of David. This, according to the dispensationalist, is one of two crucial events that will precede the second advent of Christ. The other is the rebuilding of the temple in Jerusalem on its original site. There is good reason to believe that schemes to this end have met with full approval and support on the part of many dispensationalists and that a substantial sum of money has been paid through them for the legal costs of Jewish "terrorists" arrested for plotting to dynamite the Muslim Dome of the Rock and the Al Aqsa Mosque on the temple site.

Out of such an understanding of "the fulfillment of prophecy" has grown what has been called "the cult of Israel" which identifies the biblical land of Zion with the modern state of Israel, despite the latter's secular constitutional basis and, as we have just seen, places a high value on the acquisition of the territory "bequeathed by God" as Israel's right. There are many who would confess (no doubt some dispensationalists among them) that there have been times when the cult of Israel has been given a higher priority than the expression of our common humanity.

POLITICAL FUNDAMENTALISM

The situation outlined in the preceding pages indicates that the neofundamentalist—particularly as he appears in the United States—is much more openly "a political animal" than was his predecessor of a generation or more ago who advocated "separation" rather than "involvement." During this past generation a strong bond has been formed between fundamentalist belief and political action. Not only have leading proponents of the fundamentalist position identified themselves with the policies of political figures and parties at home and in Israel itself, they at the same time have had a deep influence on those in authority, whether in government or in military circles. It is reported that President Reagan, for example, was greatly interested in dispensationalism, that he listened intently to a number of its leading exponents and showed a great personal interest in the fulfillment of prophecy such as that of Gog in Ezekiel 38 and its interpretation in terms of the Soviet Union.[19]

Christianity, I believe, cannot be isolated from politics so as to live in its own "rarefied religious atmosphere." It has to do with life as it is lived out by the people, and with the whole of life. But it does carry with it clear risks of misapplication and misinterpretation. The contents of this chapter are both a warning and a corrective. To the Christian—in the church, in the nation, and even in the state—it

---

[19]Grace Halsell's book, referred to in note 16 above, claims to give "chapter and verse" for such interest and involvement on the part of President Reagan. See also E. Glenn Hinson, "Christian Fundamentalism," in *Theology Themes*, vol. 1 no. 1 (ed. Martin Scott; Manchester: Northern Baptist College, 1992) 20–29.

really does matter how we interpret scripture, particularly prophetic and apocalyptic passages.

THE POLITICS OF THE KINGDOM

To many in authority at the time, these prophetic and apocalyptic books must have been looked upon as "political dynamite"! The Jewish leadership during the reign of Antiochus, for example, must have felt not a little apprehensive over the book of Daniel, and the Christian leadership not a little nervous over the book of Revelation. The same could be said of other apocalyptic books besides. The state authorities had perhaps good reason to hear in these religious documents distinct political overtones. They were books that castigated the rulers of the day and declared their speedy demise; these powerful leaders would be cast headlong from their thrones; they would be reduced to the level of the beast; their mighty kingdoms would be smashed in pieces and scattered to the four winds of heaven; their enemies would humiliate them; God's terrible judgment would fall upon them; their place would be taken by that small and wretched people whom they themselves had demeaned and despised; they would be made to serve this servile race until the end of time.

Such words could hardly be described as reassuring to those in power! Revelationary they might claim to be; revolutionary they most certainly were! They preached the politics of a coming kingdom whose values completely contradicted those of their lords and masters. The ruler of that kingdom was the God of the vulnerable and the victim who would ensure that justice would in the end prevail and wickedness be punished and destroyed. Even death would not provide a way of escape; the righteous martyrs would be raised to receive their reward, and the wicked would suffer torments untold (cf. Dan 12:2).

We shall examine presently how such prophecies may perhaps be more adequately tested and understood in the light of today's world. Here we simply observe, behind their exclusiveness and often vindictiveness, the expression of a hope, "eternal in the human breast," that God in his mercy will not forsake the righteous or the righteous cause but will champion the victims, the oppressed, and the marginalized and make justice prevail. The apocalyptic message is essentially a prophetic message in the sense that it addresses itself, not just to the fate of the individual in "the sweet by-and-by," but to society and the institutions of society in the here and now which also come under God's judgment. For this reason it has indeed something powerful to say to our own world with its terrible inequalities and its appalling treatment of the underprivileged and the poor. To such, says scripture, belongs the kingdom (cf. Luke 5:20ff.).

Christians are taught to pray for the coming of that kingdom "on earth as it is in heaven"—a hope confirmed by the book of Daniel and other apocalyptic writings. It is not to be confined or consigned to thousands of years hence, but to be seen at work, as Jesus' parables teach, in the here and now. It is a kingdom of righteousness and peace to be interpreted and understood, not just in spiritual, but also in political terms. It has to do with the salvation and liberation, not just of individuals from sin, but also of society from evil, corruption, oppression, and injustice of every kind.

But the apocalyptic books provide a vivid reminder that such things are to come about, not by human striving, but by the power of God. The multitiered statue in Daniel 2 is pulverized to dust by a great boulder "hewn by no human hand" (Dan 2:34 REB): the kingdom is not human-made but God-given. So too, says John in the book of Revelation, the "new Jerusalem" "comes down from God out of heaven" (Rev 21:2 REB): it is not a city built by human effort; it is a city of God's design and God's creation into which "the redeemed" may enter. Over against Jerusalem stands Babylon—a grotesque parody of the Holy City—which will be razed to the ground in God's appointed time (cf. Rev 18:2ff.) as will all other "cities," institutions, and ideologies that seek to usurp the place and the city of God.

The apocalyptic books, then, are about "the politics of God's kingdom." In the power of the Spirit, the living church in every generation is to be both the sign and the instrument of its coming.

4

PRINCIPLES AND PARADIGMS

In the preceding chapters we have looked, in broad outline, at the form and content of the biblical and extrabiblical apocalyptic literature and have examined some attempts at Christian interpretation. In this final chapter we shall first consider briefly the approach adopted by the New Testament itself; secondly, with this as our base, we shall examine certain suggested criteria which may serve as helpful guidelines for our own interpretation of the apocalyptic texts; and thirdly we shall look at a number of "affirmations of faith" made by the apocalyptic writers which may or may not have a relevance for our own generation.

INTERPRETATION IN THE NEW TESTAMENT

THE APOCALYPTIC BACKGROUND

Different assessments have been given of the place accorded to apocalyptic within the early church and the value to be placed upon it. Some see the church as an apocalyptic sect and Jesus as an apocalyptic visionary who expressed his hopes and expectations in a typically apocalyptic manner. There are others who seriously question the extent and the degree of its influence and would point to the fact, as already noted, that the book of Revelation (the only apocalypse properly so called in the New Testament) gained recognition only after much hesitation.

It seems clear from a reading of the New Testament itself and of early church history that Jesus grew up in and the early church was born into a Jewish society in which the apocalyptic world view was commonly accepted, and the apocalyptic framework of ideas was part and parcel of popular belief. The book of Revelation may indeed be the only apocalypse within the New Testament canon, but we must not make the mistake of imagining that it can be read in separation from the Gospels and the epistles that precede it. Its idiom, imagery, and symbolism may be different from theirs to a marked degree, but its message is, like theirs, founded on the revelation of scripture as a whole, Old and New Testaments together, and in so many ways is expressive of the convictions of Jesus himself, not least in its description of the eschatological hope which finds an echo, and more than an echo, in the Synoptic Gospels and in the letters of Paul (cf. 1 and 2 Thessalonians).

Jesus, we are told, came into Galilee declaring, "The time is fulfilled, and the kingdom of God is at hand" (Mark 1:15). And this was to be the recurring theme of his message. In so doing he was giving expression to a popular hope among the people that the promised day of the Lord was coming and that God's kingdom would soon be established on the earth. He spoke of that kingdom and the "mystery" of its appearing in typically apocalyptic fashion: "To you the secret of the kingdom of God has been given" (Mark 4:11 REB)—a secret whose meaning he was now revealing to his "chosen ones" just as the apocalyptic seers also did to their disciples, "the elect ones" and "the wise among the people." So central to the message of Jesus was this teaching concerning the kingdom that those first Christians, it would seem, were convinced of its speedy arrival. They would no doubt find support for such a conviction in the words of John the Baptist about "the one who was to come" (cf. Matt 3:10–12), in the promise of Jesus himself (cf. Mark 9:1; 13:30), in the earliest letter of Paul (cf 1 Thess 4:17), as well as in the book of Revelation (cf. 1:1; 22:20).[1]

The hopes of these first Christians are expressed, again in typically apocalyptic language, in such a passage as Mark 13 and its parallels in Matthew 24 and Luke 21.[2] There we read of the familiar "messianic woes" that are to precede the coming of the kingdom, and the judgment that is to follow. "As they stand," writes Norman Perrin, "the apocalyptic discourses in the New Testament are testimony to the continuing element of the apocalyptic Christianity and should be read as such."[3]

We recall too the part played in the New Testament— in both Gospels and epistles—by the eschatological struggle between "the forces of darkness" and "the forces of light." As in the Jewish apocalyptic books, the triumph of the kingdom is seen here in terms of a struggle between great cosmic powers, in which the forces of darkness, led by Satan, are ousted by the forces of light. Jesus sees Satan falling from heaven (cf. Luke 10:18) as a sign of the coming triumph, while Paul describes it as a victory over "principalities and powers" through the death and resurrection of Jesus Christ his Lord (cf. Rom 8:38ff.). The dominion, the

---

[1] Cf. Eduard Schweizer, *Jesus Christ: the Man from Nazareth and the Exalted Lord* (London: SCM, 1989) 17.
[2] Cf. Norman Perrin, "Apocalyptic Christianity," in *Visionaries,* 134ff.
[3] Ibid., 137.

victory, and the kingdom belong to him whose sovereign power is over all his works.

It is against this background and within this apocalyptic framework that we are to see Jesus' teaching concerning the coming of God's kingdom and his own part in it. The similarities between them, then, are impressive; but much more revealing are the dissimilarities. For, with penetrating spiritual insight Jesus takes up familiar concepts and transforms them completely into revelations that uniquely make known the ways and will of God.

NEW TESTAMENT PRINCIPLES OF INTERPRETATION

The actual methods of interpretation adopted by the New Testament writers are many and varied and show the influence of Jewish practice at that time.[4] These particular methods are not our concern here. We may observe, however, three principles which served as helpful criteria and which, as we shall see presently, provide useful guidelines for our own approach to the task of prophetic and apocalyptic interpretation: the New Testament writers, in their interpretation of the Old Testament, took history seriously; they took into account, not just this text and that text in isolation, but the wide sweep of biblical revelation; and they found the focus of their interpretation in the person of Jesus of Nazareth who was the fulfillment and completion of scripture.

In common with many others in their generation the first Christians, it would seem, believed that they were living in the last days and that the kingdom of God was about to break in upon them (see pp. 114ff.). But unlike the Jewish

---

[4]See C. K. Barrett, "The Interpretation of the Old Testament in the New," in *The Cambridge History of the Bible: From the Beginnings to Jerome*, vol. 1 (ed. P. R. Ackroyd and C. E. Evans; Cambridge: Cambridge University Press, 1970) ch. 12.

apocalyptic writers of their time—those "calculators of the end"—they asserted that the coming of that kingdom was not to be sought by vain calculations and speculations. Had not Jesus himself given clear warning against any such pursuits: "It is not for you to know about dates or times which the Father has set within his own control" (Acts 1:7 REB)? Or again, "You cannot tell by observation when the kingdom of God comes. You cannot say, 'Look, here it is,' or 'There it is!', for the kingdom of God is among you!" (Luke 17:20 REB). They accepted that history did indeed point beyond itself; but any such pointing forward had to be rooted in the historical event and in the operation of the sovereign Lord God on the plain of history. "The most characteristic use of scripture (in New Testament interpretation)," says C. F. D. Moule, "is 'modern' in that it treats the Old Testament as a record of revelation—as a historical narrative of God dealing with his people, to be listened to as a whole and learnt from as a continuous story. There is a world of difference between this and the use of scripture as a divining-medium."[5] The same judgment had already been made by C. H. Dodd, who saw in the New Testament's use of the Old Testament "the rudiments of an original, coherent, and flexible method of biblical exegesis" involving a view of history akin to that of the Old Testament prophets.[6] This exegesis, this "piece of genuinely creative thinking," as he calls it, cannot be the work of any of the great New Testament theologians or exegetes. The creative mind behind it can only be the mind of Jesus himself. The New Testament writers, for the most part, use scripture "historically."

As a corollary to this, they were able to take history seriously because their interpretation of scripture embraced

---

[5]C. F. D. Moule, *The Birth of the New Testament* (2d ed.; London: A. & C. Black, 1971 [1966]) 68.

[6]C. H. Dodd, *According to the Scriptures* (London: Nisbet and Co., 1952) 108f.

the whole panorama of biblical revelation as contained in the Law and the Prophets. "When in times past God spoke to our fathers, he spoke in many and various ways through the prophets" (Heb 1:1 REB). "Then starting from Moses and all the prophets, he explained to them in the whole of scripture the things that referred to himself" (Luke 24:27 REB). This last quotation gives the clue to their adoption of such an approach. There can be little doubt that they learned to interpret the Old Testament scriptures from none other than Jesus himself whose treatment, as T. W. Manson has put it, "is based on two things: a profound understanding of the essential teaching of the Hebrew scriptures and a sure judgment of his own contemporary situation."[7] Jesus' frequent reference to "so it is written" is too deeply entrenched in the Gospel strata to be other than his own as are his quotations from such a passage as Zechariah 9–14 and his dramatization of Zechariah 9:9 by riding in triumphal procession on "a colt, the foal of an ass." His interpretation of the kingdom and his own part in it was seen by him within the setting of scripture and the biblical revelation.

The third principle follows from the second and indeed from the first also. The true understanding and interpretation of scripture was to be found in Jesus of Nazareth as its fulfillment. As the apostle Peter says in his first epistle: "This salvation was the subject of intense search by the prophets who prophesied about the grace of God awaiting you. They tried to find out the time and the circumstances to which the Spirit of Christ in them pointed. . . . It was disclosed to them that these matters were not for their benefit but for yours" (1 Peter 1:10–12; cf. Heb 1:1). The mysteries recorded by the prophets, says Peter in effect, have found their true interpretation and their ultimate

[7]T. W. Manson, "The Old Testament in the Teaching of Jesus," *Bulletin of the John Rylands Library* 34 (2, 1952) 332.

fulfillment in Jesus; what the prophets blindly foretold, he and his fellow Christians now knew as a certainty. Likewise in Romans 15 Paul, with a series of Old Testament allusions, indicates how the prophets of old foretold that the Gentiles would place their hope in the Davidic Messiah—a hope which had now been realized. And again, in Acts 2:16: "This is what the prophet Joel spoke of"; and in Acts 10:43: "It is to him that all the prophets testify, declaring that everyone who trusts in him receives forgiveness of sins through his name." In Jesus the "mystery" of the kingdom (a word frequently used in the same sense in Daniel and in the Qumran texts) had become "an open secret": "To you the secret (mystery) of the kingdom of God has been given; but to those who are outside, everything comes by way of parables" (Mark 4:11f. REB).

The goal of scriptural, then, and the aim of prophetic interpretation was to discover, not this and that date or this and that circumstance governing the coming of the kingdom, but rather how the word of scripture had come to be fulfilled in Jesus. It was a fulfillment to be found not simply in the things he did (as when he rode into Jerusalem on an ass's back in fulfillment of Zech 9:9) and not simply in the things he spoke (as in his summing up of the commandments in the command to love God and to love one's neighbor as oneself), but above all in his own person as the great deliverer (through his cruel death and glorious resurrection) of whom the scriptures spoke and for whose coming the faithful so eagerly looked. The New Testament writers, then, found in Jesus of Nazareth the climax, the fulfillment of the age-long story of God's dealings with his people and they were able to do so because it was to this same conclusion that Jesus himself had come: "Everything written about me in the law of Moses and in the Prophets and Psalms was bound to be fulfilled" (Luke 24:44 REB). Starting from their own living experience of Jesus, they turned to the Old Testament and found him there as its climax, its fulfillment, or as Paul would say, "the Amen to all God's promises," for, as he says in 2 Corinthians 1:20, "All the promises of God have their Yes in him" (REB).

GUIDELINES FOR INTERPRETATION TODAY

Throughout the foregoing pages criticisms have been offered of that literalistic approach to the interpretation of prophecy and apocalyptic which, it is argued, does not take fully enough into account the "situation in life" of such writings and the symbolic and mythological language in which they are written. Note has also been taken of certain principles by means of which the New Testament writers seek to interpret the Old Testament scriptures and in particular the prophetic writings. Some of the methods they adopt reflect the Jewish background and practice in the first century A.D. and are not to be taken as a binding precedent for present-day Christians in their approach to biblical interpretation; nevertheless, having in mind the apocalyptic-world context within which the New Testament is to be understood, the three principles referred to above offer helpful guidelines in our continuing quest.

THE HISTORICAL AND CULTURAL CONTEXT

If we are to avoid the danger of purely subjective judgment and the speculation that often accompanies it, it is important to take into account the historical and cultural contexts within which the book in question was first written. A warning note of this kind needs to be sounded, if only because increasingly, it would seem, the apocalyptic text is being regarded by many as "open" or "liberated" from its context so that it can be exposed to "a transcendent interpretation." Such practice ranges from the literary critic who regards the recovery of the original context and the original audience as a vain and indeed impossible search, to the Christian fundamentalist who outdoes all others in his attempt to establish the "relevance" of the book's message, claiming that an understanding of the original message is no longer required for an understanding of its message today.

The interpretation of the book of Daniel is a particular bone of contention in this regard. If, as is commonly believed, it assumed its present form in the second century B.C. in the time of Antiochus IV Epiphanes, the book can readily be read as a commentary on the dramatic and catastrophic events that took place in Israel and in the world at large during and preceding that monarch's reign. The text illumines the events and the events elucidate the text, giving meaning to what might otherwise remain enigmatic and incomprehensible. Such an approach takes history seriously, as does scripture itself, and roots its interpretation in God's activity within the historical event in a way unlike that of purely predictive prophecy whose interpretation is often regarded as independent of the actual circumstances that brought it into being. The integrity of the text has to be recognized and upheld, and this cannot be adequately done if the historical circumstances are neglected and its original message dismissed as of no account.

Equally important in the task of interpretation is the cultural context within which the apocalyptic books were produced. It is surely of significance that in all the Jewish apocalypses of the intertestamental period, the device of pseudonymity, for example, was common practice in the presentation of "predictive prophecy," and indeed was a widely accepted style of writing in cultures well beyond the borders of Israel. It is significant too that the forms in which revelations were believed to be received—in dreams and visions, by angelic messengers, through the study of sacred texts—were all fairly stereotyped in the ancient world as indeed were the general contents of the revelations thus made known. An understanding of, say, the book of Daniel in such a setting will help us to see, not only what it has in common with other similar writings, but also what its own unique message was for its original readers; and this should make us in our day hesitate before superimposing upon it our own speculative and subjective interpretation.

It is, of course, often very difficult to ascertain with any degree of accuracy the precise "situation in life" of any book, but here the disciplines of sociology and anthropology, for example, have lent most valuable help in ascertaining the facts in terms of historical events and cultural climate. There have been great advances in this connection in recent years, and more and more evidence is readily available in scholarly books of many kinds. Help has been given too in terms of literary criticism, which has examined with care the nature of the apocalyptic genres, not only within Judaism and Christianity, but also in other diverse religions and cultures. This has cast no little light on this form of literature—its construction, its expression, its expectation, its imagery, its language, and the form of its presentation. It has become clear, as already noted, that the apocalypse was not peculiar to Jewish and Christian writings at that time but was widespread in the ancient world and followed certain fairly well-defined patterns of expression and interpretation which are to be recognized if a proper understanding of the book is to be attained. Difficult though it may be to ascertain the sociological, cultural, historical, and linguistic contexts of such books, the attempt must be made if we are to safeguard against a form of interpretation which exposes the text to misunderstanding and even to abuse. Without this anchor of historical and cultural reference the interpretation of the prophetic or apocalyptic book can all too easily drift off in any direction that takes the would-be interpreter's fancy and be made to mean almost anything he or she wants it to mean.

THE BIBLICAL REVELATION

The second principle is of equal importance: the prophetic and apocalyptic literature is to be interpreted, not in isolation from the rest as a separate class of literature, but as one expression among many of the total biblical revelation. The books of Daniel and Revelation, together with the "embryonic" apocalyptic passages embedded in the prophetic writings, belong to the canon of scripture and are to be read as such as part of the whole. Those books that lie outside the canon cannot claim the same degree of authority; but they too are to be subjected to the same test—their message is to be judged and interpreted in the light of that same total biblical revelation. And if this is true of the biblical (or nonbiblical) book, it is equally true of the biblical (or nonbiblical) "proof-text." When torn out of its biblical context (as out of its historical and cultural context), this book and that book, this verse and that verse, can be heard to say things that need to be checked by reference to the total revelation of scripture. The reader, then, will perpetrate a great injustice and the expositor will do a great disservice if he or she fails to see the apocalyptic text within the context of biblical revelation as a whole. Here is an objective test which safeguards against dogmatic assertion or ideological predilection which often tend to accompany the interpretation of books of this kind.

THE PERSON AND THE MIND OF CHRIST

For the Christian reader and expositor this will mean trying to understand these apocalyptic writings, not only in the light of the Old Testament, but also, and more importantly, in the light of the New Testament and its witness to the mind of Christ. We may take as an example

Jesus' teaching about divine judgment and the reality of the final judgment concerning which he had not a little to say. The apocalyptic writers sound the same note, but all too often their recorded revelations seem to fall far short of that of Jesus as they depict, in lurid terms and with undisguised glee, the terrible tortures and torments that will befall the enemies of God and his people.

And if this is true of the apocalyptists themselves, it is true also, it would appear, of at least some modern interpreters whose forecasting and advocacy of nuclear warfare, for example, in the name of a loving and righteous God is hard to reconcile with the revealed mind of Christ and the testimony of scripture which declares God's infinite care for his creation and his love and compassion for all men and women who dwell on the face of the earth. It is indeed curious that so many of those who claim to uphold the supreme authority of scripture, not least in its predictive prophecies, are sometimes the very people who, by their subjective interpretation and dogmatic approach, often do so much to undermine and deny the very scriptures they claim to uphold.

PREDICTION AS PARADIGM

A fourth principle may be added at this point which is implied, if not actually stated, in the New Testament. It concerns the precise nature of prediction as we find it in the prophetic and apocalyptic books. Generally speaking, such predictions are rightly to be understood in dynamic rather than in static terms, providing a paradigm for God's action in all succeeding generations. That is, the future reference has to do, not with forecasting specifically detailed events in some far distant time, but with the working out of the divine purpose in every generation; not with a predetermined plan proceeding inexorably according to some unalterable program, but a divine principle showing God at work fulfilling his divine will; not a precisely worked-out timetable of future events, but a pledge of God's presence and help, not least in times of trial. In this way the worth of books like Daniel and Revelation, for example, is not to be judged by the literal fulfillment or otherwise of their precise predictions, either in the time of Antiochus or Domitian or in our own day; it is to be judged rather by the assurance they give concerning God's final triumph over all the powers of evil. Their prophecies and predictions are of significance, "not as maps of future history, but as affirmations of the meaning of that history"; they represent "an apocalyptic paradigm from which one can conjugate a style of living"; they provide "a stimulus for the future, not simply a timetable for it."[8]

To interpret prophecy and apocalyptic in such a way is, I believe, much more "scriptural" than any literalistic approach. It takes history more seriously and recognizes more fully the incarnational character of our faith in which the word of God comes to his people within the actuality of history and supremely in the person and ministry of Jesus Christ our Lord.

When seen in such a light, the apocalyptic books assume a distinct relevance for today that otherwise they would not have. It is true that they represent a world outlook very different from our own and express themselves in language that belongs to a very different culture. But the fact remains that many of those factors that brought them into being have much in common with those that pertain in our present generation. The use of words like "apocalypse" and "apocalyptic" in today's vocabulary may be quite different in meaning, content, and

---

[8]W. Sibley Towner, "The Preacher in the Lions' Den," in *Interpreting the Prophets*, 282.

expression from their use in those early books; but the fact that they are used at all forms a bond between them that has real significance. There is in today's world a not dissimilar mood of helplessness and despair in face of oppression and war; injustice is perpetrated on every side and men and women cry out for deliverance; there is an overwhelming sense of catastrophe as rulers stretch their authority beyond the limit and scientists make possible a world devastation that those early writers could never have imagined. Men and women may no longer believe in blinding revelation and sudden divine intervention to rescue them from their dire situation; nations and peoples may not be deterred from their warlike aims by threats of a final judgment and a great trial; nevertheless, the sense of judgment is real, if only the judgment that individuals and nations bring down on their own heads. The cry for deliverance is equally real as famine strikes, disease spreads, refugees multiply, and wars rage. The very mountains seem at times to be falling on top of us! It is small wonder that "apocalyptic" is today a powerful feature in novels, films, and even computer games and is frequently to be found in the pens of journalists and on the tongues of politicians.

Two small books may be mentioned here that helpfully illustrate the dynamic and paradigmatic nature of the biblical apocalypses, Daniel and Revelation: Walter Lüthi's *The Church to Come*, an exposition of the book of Daniel written during the dark days of Hitler's rise to power in Germany, and Allan Boesak's *Comfort and Protest: Reflections on the Apocalypse of John*, written in the light of the prevailing political situation in South Africa with its heretical doctrine of apartheid.[9] Parallels are drawn respectively

---

[9]Walter Lüthi, *The Church to Come* (ET Toronto: Hodder and Stoughton and Musson, 1939); and Boesak, *Comfort and Protest*. The reader may

between the persecution of Antiochus and the oppression
of the Third Reich, and between the trials under Domitian
and the injustices perpetrated by the Pretoria regime. But
not only are the circumstances strikingly similar, the message is powerfully relevant—God has heard the protest of
his people and will honor his promise to be with them and
to save them, if not from their troubles, then in their
troubles. In their readings of Daniel and Revelation, Lüthi
and Boesak adopt a stance that is determined by "neither
the ideological dreaming of political power-brokers, nor
the fanatical fantasies of *The Late Great Planet Earth,* nor
the numerological speculation of fundamentalist schem-
ers, nor even the technical minutiae of scholars."[10] Rather,
they see in these two biblical apocalypses prophetic para-
digms that speak a powerful word to our time, a word that
has something relevant to say to politicians as well as to
preachers, a word that is more concerned about fact than
fantasy, a word that carries with it an authority that is
undiminished by the passing of the years. To read these
biblical books simply as "tracts for the times" is to deny
their prophetic power; to read them simply as speculative
forecasts is to reduce them to the level of cosmic horo-
scopes; to read them as forms of spiritual escapism into a
fantastic world of mysteries and monsters is to demean and
degrade them. They proclaim a message that is every bit as
powerful now as it was those many years ago, a message that
is at one and the same time personal and political, temporal, and eternal. What Walter Lüthi says about Daniel can
be said also about the rest of the apocalyptic books: "We
are not dealing here with a burnt-out crater. Daniel is an
active volcano. Therefore if anyone thinks that it is a matter

also wish to consult my *Daniel: An Active Volcano: Reflections on the Book
of Daniel* (Edinburgh: Saint Andrews and Philadelphia: Westminster/John
Knox, 1989.
[10] From the Foreword to Boesak, *Comfort and Protest,* 11.

of playing with cold lava, for edification or otherwise, he should realize he is playing with fire."[11]

With such things in mind, we turn in the final section to examine more fully some salient aspects of the apocalyptists' message and to see what relevance these may have for our world at this present time.

THE RELEVANCE OF APOCALYPTIC

In the opening chapter of this book the apocalyptic writings were introduced as "a perplexing literature"— and such it has proved to be! Its stilted style, its symbolic language, and its esoteric teaching all combine to confirm the judgment that it belongs to an age quite different from our own, with little or nothing in common with our own day. Its writers, it would seem, were learned individuals who give the distinct impression that their heads were in the clouds more often than their feet were on the ground!

And yet they were in no way cloistered recluses, withdrawn from the hard realities of life. On the contrary, they were those who identified themselves with their people in deeply troubled times, forced to accept the rule of foreign powers and made to suffer the indignities of a subject people—deprived of their liberties, tortured, and even martyred at the hands of tyrants.

It is a literature that asks many basic questions which succeeding generations have been asking ever since and which are every bit as apposite today as then: Why do the righteous have to suffer in the way they do? Why do tyrants have the upper hand? Where did such evil come from, and where is God in all this? What about all those promises

---

[11] Lüthi, *Church to Come*, x.

made by God in times past, pledging deliverance from their enemies? When will he act on his word and deliver his people as he said he would, and what will be the signs that the end is coming? When will the power of evil be destroyed and his promised kingdom come? What will be the final destiny of his people Israel? And what will be the lot of those righteous and those wicked individuals who, in their lifetime did not receive their proper recompense?

The apocalyptic writers set about answering these questions with an assurance that came from no mere wishful thinking but with an authority founded on divine revelation. That revelation made clear that God was on the side of the victim, that the times were in his hands, and that he would judge and save.

GOD IS SOVEREIGN LORD

Much is said in these writings, particularly in the extrabiblical books, concerning the order of creation, how its many and varied parts relate to one another, and how the whole is subject to the will of God. The entire cosmos hangs together in balance and responds in harmony to the divine word. Indeed, there is a wholeness about creation which embraces even heaven itself. Mortals may distinguish between the transient and the transcendent, the material and the spiritual, earthly might and cosmic powers, world events and heavenly portents, but to God they belong together in a wholeness which is of his creating. He made it; he sustains it; and he is in control.

Sun, moon, and stars, together with planet earth, are all part of the divine mystery which he chooses to reveal to "the wise." These heavenly bodies are much more than simply distant objects in the sky; they represent cosmic powers that exercise a profound influence on the lives of men and women and nations and are responsible for all kinds of ills on the earth. But there is no cause to be afraid;

the Lord of spirits has everything under his control. All this and much more is part of that divine mystery whose secrets are concealed in the mind of God and will one day be revealed.

And as with creation, so also with history. Just as in the so-called vertical apocalypses, such as 1 Enoch, the visionary is shown the secrets of the cosmos, so in the horizontal apocalypses, such as Daniel, he is shown the secrets of all the ages and is assured that here too God is in complete control. He is shown the full script, as it were, of that great cosmic drama that is even now being played out on the stage of history but has not as yet reached the final Act. Men and women, nations and peoples, rulers and ruled, oppressors and oppressed, angels and demons—all of these are the actors on the stage. But the sovereign Lord God is the author and director of the play! Now, for the very first time, "the plot" in its entirety is being made known.

In such a way the apocalyptic writer, even more clearly than the prophet, is able to see the whole of history as a unity. Seeing the full script, he recognizes the golden thread of God's purpose woven throughout, binding its different parts together into one. Just as God is Lord of the cosmos, so too is he Lord of history. The wholeness of space has its counterpart in the wholeness of time.

By divine revelation the writer can see that history is not only predetermined by God, it also has a distinct pattern and plan which is of God's making and is entirely under his control. Herein is one of the distinctive marks of these books—their love of systematization and schematization. History is measured and numbered and is divided into several identifiable epochs in which the rise and fall of rulers and empires is clearly depicted. The precise form of that divine pattern may vary from book to book, but it is worked out with mathematical precision, making clear that, from the very beginning, despite all appearances to the contrary, God's guiding and controlling hand has been on the long course of history and will bring it to its decreed end, an end that is now near at hand. As the writer of 2 Baruch puts it: "The youth of this world has passed away, and the power of creation is already exhausted, and the coming of the times is very near and has passed by. And the pitcher is near the well, and the ship to the harbor, and the journey to the city, and life to its end" (2 Bar. 85:10). The whole of history, like the whole of creation, has a purpose, a design, and a goal. Even the tragedies and catastrophes that face God's people are part of the great drama and will be seen to fall into place at the time of "the end" when all will be revealed.

The apocalyptic writings are not the gospel and, in their schematizations and prognostications, leave much to be desired. But their worth is to be found, not in the method they adopt, but in the message they proclaim. God is in control; he will bring to pass what he has promised and bring to naught the designs of evildoers.

EVIL IS ENDEMIC IN THE COSMOS BUT WILL BE OVERCOME

The apocalyptic writers took seriously the problem of evil. This is hardly surprising when we consider the times in which they lived and the evils they and their nation had to endure.

In some earlier books, like 1 Enoch and Jubilees, an attempt is made to explain the origin of evil in terms of the "fall" of angels called "Watchers" who "lusted after the daughters of men" (cf. 1 Enoch 6:1ff.; Jub. 5:1ff.), and from whose unholy alliance "great giants" were born who committed all kinds of sins against God. These giants are called "evil spirits" as are the creatures that emerge from their bodies after death (cf. 1 Enoch 15:3, 9f.). This evil brood has taken control of the earth, and indeed the whole cosmos, and is responsible for the many natural tragedies and catastrophes that afflict humankind—earthquakes and floods, blighted crops and unnatural births, war and disease, erupting volcanoes and storms at sea, and a multitude of other ills besides.

These "cosmic powers" (for such they are) are not to be explained simply in terms of "natural phenomena"; they are evil spirits to be identified as demons under the leadership of the Prince of Demons, Satan himself who, with all his demonic hordes, like a great army of occupation, has taken possession of the earth. Called by many different names—Beliar, Semjaza, Mastema, and the rest—Satan continues to resist God and all the host of heaven, but in the end he will be destroyed and with him all his demonic powers.

In later books such as 4 Ezra and 2 Baruch no reference is made to evil angelic powers as the cause of human sin and the evils that arise from it. Such evils are to be traced back rather to Adam's "fall" and to the choice that human beings are called upon to make between "the evil inclination" and "the good inclination" to be found in all of us. In yet other books, such as 1 Enoch 90–105, though the part played by fallen angels is recognized, people are held responsible for their wrongdoing: "Sin has not been exported into the world; it is the people themselves who have invented it" (1 Enoch 98:4). The sage Ben Sira goes further: "When the ungodly person curses Satan, he is (really) cursing himself." Whatever its origin and whatever its cause, evil is endemic in the world. But on the great day of judgment evil humans and demonic powers alike will come under the judgment of God. Satan and his angels will be destroyed, and kings will be cast down from their thrones.

Such judgment will fall most heavily on those who, in their arrogance, take upon themselves powers that belong to God alone. Such people and their evil empires are depicted in Daniel and Revelation as fearsome beasts—the very embodiment of the Evil One himself—who act with overweening pride and trample the righteous beneath their feet. Rulers like Nebuchadnezzar, Antiochus, and Domitian come in for the most severe criticism and come under the most awful judgment of God. For all such leaders "the writing is on the wall" (Dan 5:5–9); or, to change the metaphor, they have been "weighed in the balance and found wanting" (Dan 5:24–28). Once more, the Most High God is seen to be in complete control. "Judgment in history," writes Herbert Butterfield, "falls heaviest on those who come to think themselves gods, who fly in the face of Providence and history, who put their trust in human-made systems and worship the work of their own hands, and who say that the strength of their own right arm gave them the victory."[12] A timely warning!

However it is to be explained, the mystery of evil remains. The apocalyptists did not have the answer. Nevertheless, they made a valuable contribution to its final resolution. Evil is not to be explained simply in terms of my individual act of sinning; it is to be found also in societies, organizations, and institutions which are at enmity with God. But this does not mean that Satan is to be blamed and we ourselves excused. Men and women are accountable for their own sins; and sin in the human heart, like satanic evil in society, must come under the judgment of God. A relevant message indeed!

THE END IS AT HAND

Frequent reference is made throughout the apocalyptic books to the coming of "the end." The device of pseudonymity gives the impression that, from the standpoint of the assumed writer, it is a long way ahead. But in fact, from the standpoint of the reader and the apocalyptic writer himself, it is almost upon them. The end is at hand.

---

[12] H. Butterfield, *Christianity and History* (London: G. Bell and Sons, 1949) 60.

The subject of "eschatology"—the doctrine of "the last things"—has a particular fascination for these writers. The coming day of the Lord, which the prophets had foretold, will be a day of judgment, the great event towards which the whole of creation and the whole of history have been moving. The nations will be judged and stripped of their power (cf. Dan 7:12); the wicked will receive their deserts; the whole earth will be convulsed and share with individuals and nations the pangs of "the birth of the kingdom."

Then will come the time for which the long ages have been waiting. It is a time when all things will reach their consummation; evil will be destroyed and good prevail; Satan will be routed and God will reign supreme; the entire cosmos will be set free from its trammelling bonds; men and women will be transformed; history will be transcended; the whole material universe will be made new; the new heavens and the new earth of which the prophets again had spoken will be ushered in; the end will be as the beginning, and paradise will be restored.

This is an expression of faith in which the early church also shared. The apostle Paul, for example, asserts that "the whole creation has been groaning in travail together until now" (Rom 8:22). The reconciliation wrought by Christ on the cross, he says elsewhere, is a reconciliation of "all things, whether on earth or in heaven" (Col 1:20 REB). It is a reconciliation of cosmic proportions in which the creation itself will at last know the wholeness of God's salvation.

The panorama here presented by the apocalyptists and shared by the apostle Paul would seem to have little, if anything, in common with that of, say, the modern scientist searching for the origin and demise of creation. And yet, in a sense, they are asking somewhat the same basic questions. Apocalyptist and scientist, in different ways, is concerned with the order of creation, its final destiny, and the possibility of a new creation.

In the "chaos theory" of science, design can be seen even in chaos whereby the future can be predicted (albeit on a limited scale) by reference to "chaos patterns." The apocalyptist too sees "chaos patterns" which can be used, with greater boldness than in science, to predict the years ahead, patterns not only in history but also in creation itself; the apocalyptist sees in the apparently random movements of wind, rain, hail, and cloud clear evidence of God's overall design and evident signs of what is yet to be. The scientist speaks too of the earth's final destruction. To the apocalyptist it is to be by fire and water; to the scientist it is by a reversal of "the big bang" in what he is pleased to call "the big crunch"! Their language is different, they reflect totally different cultures and live in completely contrasting civilizations; and yet their goals have much in common as they pursue the meaning of the universe and the destiny of all created things.

But the eschatological concern of the apocalyptist is not confined to the fate of creation; it is concerned also with the destiny of men and women in life beyond death. In their teaching concerning the resurrection of the dead, the apocalyptists did much to pioneer the way in finding a better understanding of this age-long mystery of death. They grapple with the relationship between life and death, between the physical body and the spiritual body, and describe both life and afterlife in what we today would call psychosomatic terms. The resurrection body of which they write is not indeed a resuscitated physical body, but it is a body nonetheless whose "ground-plan," as it were, is closely related to the body of flesh and blood. As with the emergence of the new creation following "cosmic death," so with the emergence of the new person following physical death. The resurrection body form is different from the old, but it does not signify its total abolition. Human life, expressed in terms of body is, as it were, the "raw material" from which the new emerges. The apocalyptic writers would not have used such language to express their belief in the state of survival beyond death, but within the limitations of their mythological understanding they pose the same basic questions as the modern theologians for which they claim to have found an answer in terms of the mercy and the judgment of God.

The relevance of this to the New Testament accounts of the resurrection of Jesus, to what is said about his resurrection body and to the spiritual body referred to by the apostle Paul, is obvious. Apocalyptist and New Testament writer alike belonged to a generation and a culture in which basic questions concerning life and death were commonplace. The gospel claims that, in the resurrection of Jesus, surmise becomes certainty and the resurrection hope becomes a realizable and realized hope, not only for the individual but also for the whole universe in whose redemption all things will be made new.

The apocalyptist, it is true, indulges in much speculation concerning the destruction of creation, by fire and brimstone and by devastating flood, and concerning human survival, with its description of what has been called "the furniture of heaven and the temperature of hell"! Often such speculation runs riot in a display of outlandish fantasy. But even here the apocalyptist may have at least something in common with both the scientist and the theologian who, it may be said, in their cosmological and eschatological explanations, also indulge at times in surmise and speculation every bit as extensive as that of the visionary of old!

The summing up of all things in Christ, then, marks the end, and the end marks a new beginning—the breaking in of God's kingdom in which the living and the dead will participate. It is a momentous event which finds focus in the Christian hope of the parousia, the appearing of the Lord in his second advent. In the book of Revelation and elsewhere in the New Testament this hope is expressed in specifically apocalyptic terms and is given an established place in the church's message of salvation. In his coming kingdom God the creator will be seen as God the redeemer.

THE KINGDOM IS COMING

The promise of prophecy and apocalyptic alike was that the kingdom was coming and was coming soon! In the apocalyptic writings this great hope found kaleidoscopic expression: but one thing was clear—the Lord God would intervene to save his people; the powers of darkness would be destroyed, and his unending rule of righteousness and peace would be established.

This same hope was central too in the teaching and ministry of Jesus. "The time is fulfilled," he says at the very beginning of his public ministry, "and the kingdom of God is at hand; repent and believe in the gospel" (Mark 1:15). As visionaries scanned the heavens or scoured their sacred books for signs of its appearing, Jesus announced, "The kingdom of God is in the midst of you" (Luke 17:21). At long last the kingdom had come and was established here on the earth! It was present in the person and work of Jesus of Nazareth. That was Jesus' own conviction as well as the conviction of the early church; the kingly rule of God had found visible expression in him!

It is a claim that is supported, not only by the teaching of his parables, but also by his miracles of healing, not least those involving the exorcism of evil spirits. These are more than simply acts of physical or mental healing such as a physician might perform; they are presented in the Gospels as evident signs of his victory over those cosmic powers of evil entrenched in the world. Those people who had been bound hand and foot by Satan were now being set free. Satan had been defeated and the age of salvation had begun. What is more, in this victory his disciples were privileged to share: "Lord, even the demons are subject to us in your name," to which Jesus replied, "I saw Satan fall like lightning from heaven" (Luke 10:17f.). Satan's days are numbered; he is even now being stripped of his power; his house is already plundered (cf. Matt 12:29).

But the coming of the kingdom in Jesus is heralded, not only in his teaching and in his miracles, but above all in his death on the cross and in his resurrection. Here is something the apocalyptic writers could not have foreseen, the cruciform shape of the kingdom—not a barbed arrow, but a rugged cross. To them a "crucified Messiah" was a contradiction in terms. But to Jesus and his followers Calvary was no mere "accident of history," nor was it simply one more illustration of "human inhumanity." In his cross, they believed, he had triumphed over "principalities and powers" (cf. Col 2:15 margin). Satan had been defeated (cf. Heb 3:14), and "the age to come" had at last dawned (cf. Heb 6:5).

And with the cross went the resurrection. The cross, says John, is Christ's "glorification"; and the resurrection is a manifestation and confirmation of his triumph there, an open demonstration that "the Lamb who was slain" is "the Lamb upon the throne" (Rev 5:6) to whom belong "the kingdom, the power and the glory for ever." To the apocalyptist, the resurrection was something to be expected at the end of time. The Christian church believed—and believes—that already in Jesus it had taken place and that he was "the firstfruits of the harvest of the dead" (1 Cor 15:20 REB). In his resurrection the kingdom was seen to come "with power" (Mark 9:1; Rom 1:4)—a power that was made manifest on the day of Pentecost when, in fulfillment of Joel's prophecy (cf. 2:28; Acts 2:17), the spirit "in the last days" would be poured out on "all flesh." That great day had at last come. Henceforth the followers of Jesus, his church, in the power of the Spirit would stand as both sign and instrument of the kingdom throughout the earth.

But even that is not the complete picture. The kingdom is indeed present in Jesus and is being made visible by the operation of the Holy Spirit in and through his church; but it still awaits its consummation.

> The tension between the "now" and the "not yet" shows itself already in prophetic and apocalyptic expectation. But whereas in such writers these two aspects were held together in balance, in the ministry of Jesus they were held together in tension in such a way that the blessings of the coming kingdom became a present possession, the passive expectation a dynamic experience. In this tension Jesus' followers had to wait and watch and pray. They were at one and the same time a witnessing community immersing themselves in the life of their society as they made known the good news of Jesus, and an eschatological community "awaiting our blessed hope, the appearing of the glory of our great God and Savior Jesus Christ" (Titus 2:13).[13]

"It is in this peculiar tension between the future and the present that Jesus introduces a novel element ultimately destructive of the apocalyptic framework."[14] When the apocalyptists claimed that the kingdom was at hand, they spoke of its nearness in time; when Jesus proclaimed the same message, he spoke, not just in terms of its immediacy, but also in terms of its urgency. The presence of the kingdom was a penetrating force, powerful and effective in the here and now. The early church looked forward eagerly to the second coming of their Lord, when his kingdom would be recognized and everything in heaven and on earth and "under the earth" would acknowledge him as Lord. But it is most significant that early believers did not spend their time gazing wistfully into the heavens or speculating endlessly, with the help of either the stars or the scriptures, concerning the time or the manner of his appearing, despite their temptation to do so (cf. Acts 1:11). Rather, this "glorious hope" galvanized them into action in their witness to their Lord, both in the words they spoke and in the lives they lived. They drew strength, not

---

[13] D. S. Russell, *Poles Apart* (Edinburgh: Saint Andrews, 1990) 134ff.
[14] Lewis S. Ford, The Lure of God (Philadelphia: Fortress, 1978) 35.

just from their remembrance of the past when Jesus was with them in the flesh, but also from their "remembrance of the future" when he would reign. The coming Christ and the coming kingdom are not just an empty, pious hope. They are a powerful hope that makes sense of both past and present and assures us that the victory belongs even now to "our God and his Christ." "In this hope," says Paul, "we are saved. Now hope that is seen is not hope. For who hopes for what he sees? But if we hope for what we do not see, we wait for it with patience" (Rom 8:24f.).

The Jewish apocalyptic writers, in their declaration of the coming kingdom, prophesied more than they ever realized. It is true that, in their understanding of divine revelation and in their expression of it, they fall far short of the New Testament; and their affirmations of faith lack the certainty and the maturity of a John, a Peter, or a Paul. Nevertheless, for their contribution to that "preparation for the gospel" to which the Old Testament itself also bears witness—not least in its prophetic and apocalyptic books—and for their abiding message concerning the sovereign rule of Almighty God, they surely claim a worthy place in the Jewish and Christian heritage and deserve greater honor than they have often been given in the past.

A SELECT BIBLIOGRAPHY

Boesak, Allan A. *Comfort and Protest: Reflections on the Apocalypse of John of Patmos.* Edinburgh: Saint Andrews, 1987.

Clouse, Robert G., ed. *The Meaning of the Millennium: Four Views,* with contributions by George Eldon Ladd, Herman A. Hoyt, Loraine Boettner, and Anthony A. Hoekema. Downers Grove, Ill.: InterVarsity, 1977.

Cohn, Norman. *The Pursuit of the Millennium: Revolutionary Millenarians and Mystical Anarchists of the Middle Ages.* Revised and Expanded Edition. New York: Oxford University Press, 1970.

Collins, J. J. *Daniel, with an Introduction to Apocalyptic Literature.* Grand Rapids: Eerdmans, 1984.

_____. *The Apocalyptic Imagination: An Introduction to the Jewish Matrix of Christianity.* New York: Crossroad, 1984.

_____. "Apocalyptic Literature." In *Early Judaism and its Modern Interpreters.* Edited by R. A. Kraft and G. W. E. Nickelsburg. Philadelphia: Fortress and Atlanta: Scholars, 1986.

Halsell, Grace. *Prophecy and Politics: Militant Evangelists on the Road to Nuclear War.* Westport, Conn.: Lawrence Hill & Co., 1986.

Hanson, P. D. *Old Testament Apocalyptic.* Interpreting Biblical Texts. Nashville: Abingdon, 1987.

Koch, K. *The Rediscovery of Apocalyptic.* London: SCM, 1972.

Lacocque, André. *Daniel in His Time.* Columbia: University of South Carolina Press, 1988.

Lindsey, Hal. *The Late Great Planet Earth.* Grand Rapids: Zondervan, 1970.

_____. *There's a New World Coming.* Irvine, Calif.: Harvest House, 1973 and Coverdale House, 1974.

_____. *Satan is Alive and Well on Planet Earth.* Grand Rapids: Zondervan, 1972 and London: Marshall, Morgan & Scott, 1973.

Lüthi, Walter. *The Church to Come.* Toronto: Hodder & Stoughton and Husson, 1939.

Nicholson, E. W. "Apocalyptic." In *Tradition and Interpretation. Essays by Members of the Society for Old Testament Study.* Edited by G. W. Anderson. Pages 189-213. Oxford: Clarendon, 1979.

Nickelsburg, George W. E. *Jewish Literature Between the Bible and the Mishnah.* Philadelphia: Fortress, 1981.

Reese, Alexander. *The Approaching Advent of Christ: an Examination of the Teaching of J. N. Darby and His Followers.* London and Edinburgh: Marshall, Morgan & Scott, 1937.

Rist, M. "Apocalypticism." In *Interpreter's Dictionary of the Bible.* Volume 1. Pages 157ff. Nashville: Abingdon, 1962.

Rowley, H. H. *The Relevance of Apocalyptic.* 3d ed. London: Lutterworth, 1963.

Russell, D. S. *Apocalyptic: Ancient and Modern.* London: SCM and Philadelphia: Fortress, 1978.

_____. *Daniel. An Active Volcano.* Edinburgh: Saint Andrew and Philadelphia: Westminster/John Knox, 1989.

_____. *Divine Disclosure: an Introduction to Jewish Apocalyptic.* London: SCM and Philadelphia: Fortress, 1992.

Towner, W. Sibley. *Daniel.* Interpretation: A Biblical Commentary for Teaching and Preaching. Atlanta: John Knox, 1984.

INDEX OF SUBJECTS

INDEX OF AUTHORS

INDEX OF TEXTS

Granulated Sugar (caster sugar)

¼ cup = 55g = 4 tbsp
75g   = 6 tbsp
⅓ cup   = 90g
½ cup   = 120g
¾ cup   = 175g
1 cup   = 225g
1¼ cups   = 275g
1½ cups   = 350g
2 cups   = 450g

Confectioner's Sugar (icing sugar)

¼ cup   = 25g
½ cup   = 55g
1 cup   = 120g
1½ cups   = 175g
1¾ cups   = 225g

Flour

¼ cup   = 25g
½ cup   = 55g
⅓ cup   = 75g
¾ cup   = 100g
1 cup   = 120g
1¼ cups   = 145g
1½ cups   = 175g
1¾ cups   = 200g
2 cups   = 225g
2¼ cups   = 250g
2½ cups   = 275g
3 cups   = 350g
3½ cups   = 400g
4 cups   = 450g
4¼ cups   = 500g
6½ cups   = 750g

Dairy

1 cup   = 120g grated hard cheese
¾ cup   = 185g cream cheese
1 cup   = 225g cream cheese
¾ cup   = 55g grated Parmesan
1 cup   = 85g grated Parmesan
½ cup   = 125g yogurt or sour cream
¾ cup   = 175g yogurt or sour cream
1 cup   = 250g yogurt or sour cream
½ cup   = 115g mayonnaise
1 cup   = 225g mayonnaise

Breadcrumbs

1 cup   = 65g dried
2 cups   = 130g dried
4 cups   = 250g dried
1 cup   = 55g fresh

Dry Ingredients

1 cup   = 225g rice
1 cup   = 200g rolled oats
¼ cup   = 40g ground almonds
¼ cup   = 25g sliced almonds
1 cup   = 150g peanuts
1 cup   = 120g chopped nuts
¾ cup   = 75g cornmeal
1 cup   = 150g raisins
1 cup   = 250g dried beans
2 cups   = 500g dried beans

the way to a
Man's Heart

liz wolf-cohen

the way to a
Man's Heart

romantic recipes for every occasion

Liz Wolf-Cohen

MQP

fisherman's catch 10

Published by MQ Publications Limited
12 The Ivories
6-8 Northampton Street
London N1 2HY
Tel: +44 (0)20 7359 2244
Fax: +44 (0)20 7359 1616
email: mail@mqpublications.com
website: www.mqpublications.com

Copyright © MQ Publications Limited 2002

Text: Copyright © 2002 Liz Wolf-Cohen
Editor: Yvonne Deutch
Design: Lindsey Johns, Design Revolution

ISBN: 1-84072-469-2

10 9 8 7 6 5 4 3 2 1

Printed and bound in China

rib-stickin' good meal 60

man-size snacks

what's for supper darling?

contents

hunky crunchy 'n fresh

sweets for your sweetie

Introduction

When we look back to the bygone days of the 1950s, the images and feelings evoked are immensely powerful and memorable. It's as if those years represent a far-off golden age when men went out to work and women stayed at home to be full-time mothers and homemakers. What's more, while these ultra-feminine ladies were busy doing the cooking they wore enticingly pretty, frilly aprons and big, bright, beaming smiles. They also had smart, newly equipped kitchens, well stocked pantries and refrigerators, and a repertoire of delicious recipes that filled the air with the wonderful aromas of home cooking.

It was these recipes that gave every 50s woman worthy of her pinafore an unerring pathway to her man's heart. "What's for supper, darling?" When she heard this plaintive request, she knew exactly what to serve up! She cooked her man rib-sticking, tasty meals that made him come back for more every time. It was food that can only be described as 'retro cooking'—meatloaves, thick hearty soups, steaming casseroles of beef, lamb or chicken, fried chicken with mashed potatoes—dishes that produce glowing feelings of warmth and security in a guy:

You can discover the same, old fashioned route to masculine affections in *The Way to a Man's Heart*. Substantial dishes such as Deep Dish Chicken Pot Pie, Southern-Fried Chicken and Beef Stew with Herb Dumplings will wrap your man up in a warm blanket of tender loving care; and he'll adore these no-nonsense suppers of Corned Beef Hash and Eggs, Franks and Beans and Baked Macaroni and Cheese. Simple, tasty snacks are a great hit too—there's nothing quite like a well made Chili Dog, Cheeseburger or Italian Submarine Sandwich. You'll also discover the secret love that many men harbor for sweets and desserts. He'll love you forever when he tastes your mouth watering Double-Crust Apple Pie and Hot Fudge Sundae, and he'll think that you really are an angel when you serve up a light-as-air Angel Food Cake

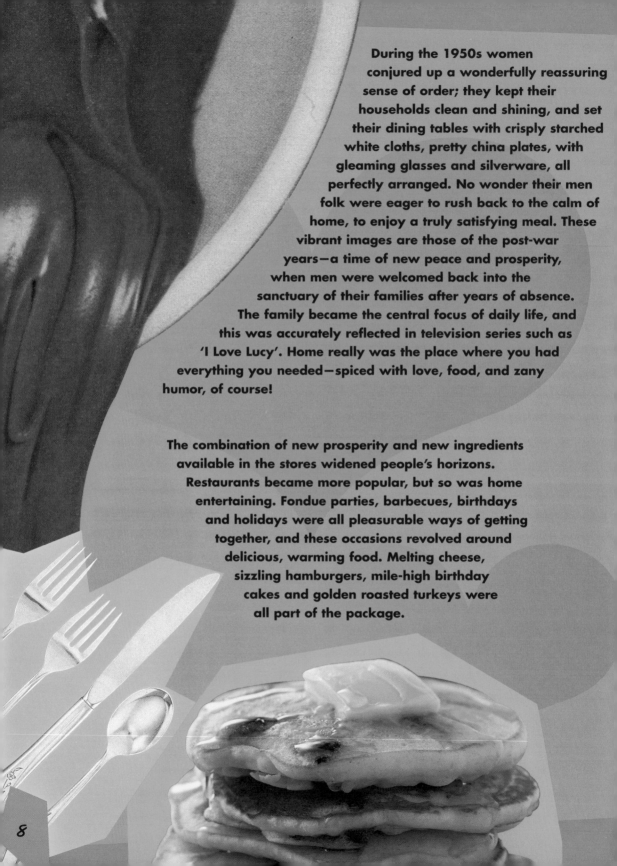

During the 1950s women conjured up a wonderfully reassuring sense of order; they kept their households clean and shining, and set their dining tables with crisply starched white cloths, pretty china plates, with gleaming glasses and silverware, all perfectly arranged. No wonder their men folk were eager to rush back to the calm of home, to enjoy a truly satisfying meal. These vibrant images are those of the post-war years—a time of new peace and prosperity, when men were welcomed back into the sanctuary of their families after years of absence. The family became the central focus of daily life, and this was accurately reflected in television series such as 'I Love Lucy'. Home really was the place where you had everything you needed—spiced with love, food, and zany humor, of course!

The combination of new prosperity and new ingredients available in the stores widened people's horizons. Restaurants became more popular, but so was home entertaining. Fondue parties, barbecues, birthdays and holidays were all pleasurable ways of getting together, and these occasions revolved around delicious, warming food. Melting cheese, sizzling hamburgers, mile-high birthday cakes and golden roasted turkeys were all part of the package.

In these turbulent times, it's a relief to return to this glowing vision of what's really important—love, family, home, friends, and security. It seems that all of us, men especially, seem to need that magical feeling of being at home with a satisfying bowl of spaghetti and meatballs, or homemade chicken soup. You can keep that magic alive for your man by giving him what he really wants— delicious dishes that will prove to you that food truly is *The Way to a Man's Heart.*

fisherman's catch

These divine fish dishes will net in your dream
guy, and will keep him hooked on your cooking
forever. While Clams Casino will appeal to the
dashing hero image every man secretly
believes he can achieve, tempting Shrimp
Cocktails or Luxurious Lobster Thermidor
will reveal his romantic side over a dinner
à deux. When all he wants is a little caring
and sharing, Clam Chowder or Tuna Noodle
Casserole are the dishes to make every
man feel loved and wanted.

New England Clam Chowder

There's nothing like the flavor of fresh clams—they're just so delicious. If your man has brought back a good haul from the beach, make him a pan of this fragrant, creamy soup. He'll really love it.

Serves 6

4oz/120g salt pork or thick rindless
   bacon slices (rashers), diced
2 onions, chopped
36 clams, shucked, with their liquid
2 tbsp all-purpose (plain) flour
3 large potatoes, diced
1 tbsp chopped fresh thyme or
   1/2 tsp dried thyme
2 1/2 cups/600ml milk
1/2 cup/125ml whipping cream
salt and freshly ground black or
   white pepper

1 Cook the salt pork or bacon in a large heavy-based saucepan or casserole over medium heat until golden. Add the onions and cook for about 5 minutes, stirring frequently, until softened.

2 Measure the clam liquid and add enough water to make it up to 2 cups/500ml. Sprinkle the flour over the bacon and onion mixture in the pan and stir until it is evenly mixed, then cook for about 1 minute. Gradually whisk in the clam liquid until smooth and bring to the boil, whisking until slightly thickened.

3 Add the potatoes and thyme, and season with salt and pepper. Reduce the heat and simmer, covered, for 15 minutes or until the potatoes are just tender.

4 Meanwhile, coarsely chop the clams and add to the pan with the milk. Cover the pan and cook for a further 10 minutes.

5 Stir in the cream, taste and adjust the seasoning. Heat the chowder gently for 5 minutes before serving hot.

Clams Casino

Clams are a surprisingly versatile seafood and they can be cooked in a variety of ways, in chowders or grilled, as they are here. In the 1960s clambakes were the fashionable and fun way to feast on the beach.

4–6 rindless bacon slices (rashers),
  cut into small pieces
2 green (spring) onions, finely chopped
1 small green bell pepper, seeded and finely
  chopped
1 celery stalk, finely chopped
1–2 tbsp lemon juice
2–3 tbsp chopped parsley
2–3 dashes Worcestershire sauce
24 clams, on the half shell
dried bread crumbs, for sprinkling
rock salt or foil, for cooking
salt and freshly ground black pepper

1 Cook the bacon in a frying pan over low heat until the fat begins to melt. Increase the heat to medium and cook until the bacon is crisp and golden. Drain on paper towels.

2 Pour off all but 1 tablespoon fat from the pan and return it to the heat. Add the green onions, pepper and celery, and cook gently for about 5 minutes, stirring, until the vegetables are softened. Stir in the lemon juice and parsley, and season with the Worcestershire sauce and salt and pepper. Remove from the heat and leave to cool slightly.

3 Preheat the broiler (grill). Spread the rock salt thickly over the base of a flameproof dish or the broiler tray. Alternatively, crumple sheets of foil to make a cushion to hold the clam shells upright.

4 Use a teaspoon to top each clam with some vegetable mixture, sprinkle lightly with bread crumbs and arrange in rows on the rock salt or foil. Push the shells gently into the salt or foil to steady them.

5 Broil (grill) the clams for about 10 minutes, until the vegetable mixture is golden and the clams are just cooked. Serve hot, on a bed of fresh rock salt or crumpled foil.

Shrimp (Prawn) Cocktails

Serves 4

Give your guy a welcome change with this 50s classic. A simple, delicious appetizer, this tasty treat is experiencing a well-deserved revival.

1lb/450g peeled cooked medium
  shrimp (prawns), deveined,
  with tails if possible
4 crisp lettuce leaves,
  such as iceberg
lemon wedges or twists, to garnish

Cocktail Sauce
1/2 cup/125ml tomato
  ketchup
1/2 cup/125ml chili sauce
2–3 tsp bottled horseradish
1 1/2–2 tsp lemon juice

1 First prepare the cocktail sauce by mixing all the ingredients in a small bowl. Cover and chill.

2 Arrange the lettuce leaves on four plates. Divide the shrimp equally among the plates and spoon over a little sauce.

3 Garnish the cocktails with lemon wedges or twists. Serve any remaining sauce separately.

Beer-Battered Shrimp (Prawns)

Serves 4-6

Shrimp (prawns) are a universally popular shellfish —they're utterly delicious whether they are eaten simply boiled, or deep fried in batter, as they are here. The beer in this batter makes a light, crisp coating.

1½–2lb/675–900g large raw shrimp (prawns), peeled and deveined, with tails if possible
vegetable oil, for deep-frying

Beer Batter
¾ cup/120g all-purpose (plain) flour
1½ tsp salt
¾–1 cup/185–250ml beer

Garnish
lemon wedges
parsley sprigs

16

1 Rinse and dry the shrimp well with paper towels.

2 Sift the flour into a bowl and stir in the salt. Using a fork, gradually stir in the beer—do not over-mix the batter as a few lumps of flour will not matter.

3 Heat the oil for deep-frying to 375°F/190°C over medium-high heat. Using your fingers or tongs and working in batches, dip the shrimp into the batter and then drop them into the hot oil. Cook for about 1 minute, until crisp and golden,

turning once. Drain on paper towels and keep hot until all the shrimp are battered and cooked.

4 Arrange the shrimp in a napkin-lined basket or bowl and garnish with lemon wedges and parsley sprigs.

Tuna Noodle Casserole

Good old comfort food, this popular casserole supper satisfied many a man's hunger during the retro era. Sometimes it is made with canned soup as a base, but why not try this version made with home-made white sauce—it is creamy and delicious.

Serves 6-8

6 tbsp/90g butter or margarine
1 onion, finely chopped
2 stalks celery, thinly sliced
½ tsp dried thyme
4 tbsp all-purpose (plain) flour
3 cups/750ml milk
½ cup/125g sour cream (optional)
6oz/175g mushrooms, sliced and lightly
  sautéed in butter
6oz/175g frozen peas, thawed
8oz/225g egg noodles, cooked and drained
2 x 7oz/190g cans tuna, drained
4 tbsp dried bread crumbs
salt and freshly ground black pepper

1 Preheat the oven to 350°F (180°C/Gas 5). Melt 4 tbsp/60g of the butter in a large, heavy-based saucepan over medium heat. Add the onion, celery and thyme and cook, stirring frequently, for about 5 minutes, until the vegetables are softened.

2 Stir in the flour and cook, stirring frequently, for about 2 minutes, until well blended. Season with salt and pepper.

3 Gradually whisk in the milk and cook until the sauce thickens and begins to boil. Reduce the heat to low and simmer for about 10 minutes, stirring frequently. If the sauce becomes too thick, add a little more milk. Remove from the heat and stir in the sour cream.

4 Add the mushrooms, peas, and noodles, and flake in the tuna. Toss well to combine and turn into a large baking dish, then spread the mixture out evenly.

5 Melt the remaining butter in a small frying pan over medium heat. Add the bread crumbs and stir to coat completely, then sprinkle the mixture evenly over the casserole.

6 Bake for about 25 minutes, until the top is crisp and golden and the casserole is bubbling. Serve immediately.

Crab Louis

When you can get some fresh crab at the fishmonger, make him this famous classic. Crab Louis originated in a San Francisco hotel around the 1900s. It became universally popular in the 1950s and has remained so ever since.

Serves 4

1 head soft or butterhead lettuce, leaves
  separated, washed, and dried
1–1½lb/ 450–675g white crabmeat,
  picked over
4 hard-cooked eggs, halved
8 cherry tomatoes, halved
20 black olives, preferably Niçoise or
  herb-dried
1 tbsp chopped dill, to garnish

Dressing

1 cup/225g mayonnaise

1 tbsp lemon juice

1/2 small onion, grated

1/2 green bell pepper, seeded
  and minced or finely chopped

1/4 cup/60ml sweet or hot chili sauce,
  or to taste

1 tsp Worcestershire sauce

1 First make the dressing: put the mayonnaise in a bowl and stir in the lemon juice, onion, pepper, chile and Worcestershire sauces until well blended. Set aside.

2 Arrange the lettuce leaves on four plates. Mound equal amounts of crabmeat in the middle and arrange the hard-cooked eggs and tomato halves around the crab.

3 Sprinkle the olives over the top and spoon over some of the dressing. Sprinkle with dill to garnish and serve the remaining dressing separately.

Lobster Thermidor

He'll be most gratified if you pamper him with this fabulous dish. It is French in origin, but became widely popular after World War II. Then, **Serves 2—4** along with Lobster Newburg, it could be found on every continental-style restaurant menu in big cities and replicated in many homes for fancy dinner parties.

2 live lobsters (about 2lb/900g each)
2 tbsp/30g butter
2 tbsp all-purpose (plain) flour
½ cup/125ml milk
2 tbsp brandy
½ cup/125ml heavy (double)
    or whipping cream
1 tbsp Dijon mustard
cayenne pepper
squeeze of lemon juice
a little grated Parmesan cheese,
    for sprinkling
salt and freshly ground white pepper
parsley sprigs, to garnish

1 Bring a large saucepan or stockpot three-quarters full of salted water to a boil over high heat. Gently drop the lobsters head first into the water, cover and return the water to a boil. Reduce the heat to medium and simmer for about 8 minutes. Lift the lobsters out and place on a rack to drain and cool slightly.

2 Set the lobsters on their backs on a board. Using a large, heavy knife and beginning at the head, split the lobsters lengthwise in half. Discard the blackish sac behind the eyes. If you like, reserve the green liver (tomalley) and the roe (coral) for the sauce. Remove all the meat from the shell and devein the tail. Crack the claws and remove the meat; cut it into bite-size pieces and set aside. Rinse the shell halves and dry with paper towels, then set aside.

3 Melt the butter over medium-high heat in a heavy-based saucepan. Stir in the flour until well blended and cook for about 1 minute, stirring. Gradually whisk in the milk to make a smooth sauce, then whisk in the brandy and cream.

4 If using the lobster liver and roe, press them through a sieve into the pan and whisk into the sauce—the liver and roe are not essential but they enrich the sauce. Reduce the heat to low and simmer for 8–10 minutes, until thick and creamy. Stir in the mustard and season with salt and pepper and a sprinkling of cayenne pepper. Add a little lemon juice. Remove from the heat and gently stir in the lobster meat.

5 Preheat the broiler (grill). Crumple a few sheets of foil and lay on to the broiler pan or in a flameproof baking dish. Press each lobster shell half into the foil to keep it steady. Carefully divide the lobster mixture evenly among the shells. Sprinkle each with a little Parmesan and broil until golden and bubbly. Garnish with parsley and serve immediately.

COOK'S TIP

Instead of cooking lobster at home,
make this dish with bought freshly
cooked lobster. Ask the fishmonger
to split and clean the lobsters.

Crispy Fish Cakes

When cod was cheap and plentiful, fish cakes were a common way of using leftover fish from Friday night's supper.

Now that cod is being fished out of existence and has become quite expensive, fish cakes are a smart treat! These are utterly delicious with tomato ketchup, mashed potatoes and a dish of fresh peas. If your man is a keen fisherman, you can make fish cakes with trout, too.

juice of 1/2 lemon

1 1/2lb/ 675g cod or other white fish,
  salmon or trout fillets or steaks

1lb/ 450g potatoes, cut into pieces

5 tbsp/ 75g butter

1 onion, finely chopped

1 large egg

1 egg yolk

2 tbsp chopped dill, chives or parsley,
  or a mixture of these herbs

dried bread crumbs, for coating

vegetable oil, for frying

salt and freshly ground black pepper

parsley or dill sprigs, to garnish

1 Bring a medium frying pan half-filled with water to a boil. Add the lemon juice and 1 teaspoon salt. Add the fish and reduce the heat to low. Simmer gently until the fish is just cooked, spooning the water over it to poach the top—it is preferable to undercook the fish slightly rather than overcook it. Drain on paper towels and cool slightly.

2 When cool enough to handle, flake the fish into a large mixing bowl, being careful to pick out any bones or skin. Press a piece of plastic wrap (cling film) or paper towel against the surface of the fish to prevent if from drying out.

3 Meanwhile, cook the potatoes in boiling salted water for about 15 minutes, until tender. Drain well and return to the pan. Using a potato masher, mash until smooth. Beat in 3 tablespoons of the butter and season with salt and pepper.

4 In a small frying pan, melt half the remaining butter over medium heat. Add the onion and cook gently for about 7 minutes, until softened. Stir into the mashed potato mixture.

5 Beat the egg, egg yolk, and chopped herbs into the potato mixture, then gently fold in the flaked fish until well blended. Taste for seasoning and, if you like, add a squeeze of lemon juice. Shape into 8 patties.

6 Put the bread crumbs in a plastic bag. Put each fish patty into the bag in turn and shake and turn to coat completely with bread crumbs. Arrange on a baking sheet and chill for at least 20 minutes.

7 Heat about 1/4 inch/5mm depth of vegetable oil in a large heavy-based frying pan. Add 1 tablespoon butter and heat over medium-high heat until the butter is melted and sizzling, then swirl to blend the butter and oil. Add the fish cakes, in batches if necessary, and cook for about 8 minutes, until golden brown on both sides, turning halfway through cooking. Drain on paper towels and serve immediately or at room temperature, garnished with the parsley or dill.

COOK'S TIP
These fish cakes can also be made with instant mashed potatoes. Follow the directions on the package using skimmed milk instead of water, and beat in the butter.

man-size snacks

Watch faces light up when you serve these all-time winners to the boys in your life. Five, fifteen, or fifty, no matter what their age, they'll wolf down Chili Dogs or Bacon Cheeseburger with Red Onion Relish with ravenous enthusiasm. When the going gets tough, and the tough are out shopping, an Italian Submarine Sandwich or a classic Club Sandwich refuel loved ones—and they're great snacks to share, too. Having a party? Check out the cheeky way guys grab the cocktail snacks when you hand around Pigs in Blankets or Deviled Eggs; they'll bring out the child in the most sophisticated man.

Club Sandwich

This superior sandwich is supposedly named after the double-decker railroad carriages known as club cars, that were the stylish travel option in the early 1900s. It is a true man-size sandwich and is still especially popular as a late-night hotel snack.

6 slices good quality white bread
butter (optional)
4–6 tbsp good quality mayonnaise
4–6 crisp lettuce leaves
2 ripe tomatoes, sliced
8 rindless bacon slices (rashers),
  cooked until crisp
6oz/175g cooked chicken breast, sliced

To Serve
bread-and-butter pickle or chutney
potato chips (crisps)

1 Lightly toast the bread. Butter each slice on one side only, if required. Lay 2 slices on a cutting board or work surface.

2 Spread each slice with mayonnaise and cover with 2 or 3 lettuce leaves; add slices of tomato, and 2 bacon slices. Top each with a second slice of toast, spread with more mayonnaise and add another lettuce leaf. Cover evenly with slices of chicken breast. Cover with the remaining slices of toast, buttered sides down.

3 Cut each sandwich into 4 triangles and secure each triangle with a toothpick. Arrange on plates and serve immediately, with the pickles and potato chips on the side.

Italian Submarine Sandwich

Depending on where folk live, this sandwich, or something like it, might be called a hero, grinder, torpedo, hoagie, poorboy, or sub. Hand your own hero one of these tasty treats when he's peckish; it's a fresh roll, layered with various deli meats (mostly Italian), salami, cheese, onions, and tomatoes. Serve with pickles or potato chips (crisps).

½ cup/115g mayonnaise
¼ cup/60g sour cream
1 tbsp Dijon mustard
4 individual French rolls,
  about 8in/20cm long
butter or margarine, softened, for spreading
crisp lettuce leaves
6oz/175g boiled or baked ham, sliced
6oz/175g salami
6oz/175g cooked chicken or turkey, sliced
4oz/120g Emmental cheese, sliced
4oz/120g Cheddar cheese, sliced
2 tomatoes, thinly sliced
1 large green bell pepper, seeded
  and cut into rings
1 onion, thinly sliced

1 In a small bowl, combine the mayonnaise, sour cream, and mustard until well blended.

2 Using a serrated knife, split the rolls horizontally in half. Remove some of the soft bread and spread both halves lightly with butter or margarine. Spread the top halves generously with the mayonnaise mixture.

3 Arrange 2–3 lettuce leaves on the bottom half of each roll, folding them to fit. Layer the remaining ingredients in order on top of the lettuce. Cover with the tops and cut across in half.

Grilled Cheese and Tomato Sandwich with Bacon

Serves 4

Actually, these sandwiches are fried. They are easily one of the most popular types of snacks, and can be quickly made at home when your man needs a tasty lunch or supper.

8 slices good quality country-style
  white bread
4 tbsp/55g butter, softened
2 tbsp Dijon mustard
4–6oz/115–175g Swiss cheese, thinly sliced
4–6oz/115–175g Cheddar cheese or
  Monterey Jack, thinly sliced
8 thick tomato slices
8 rindless bacon slices (rashers),
  cooked until crisp

To Serve

bread-and-butter pickle or chutney
potato chips (crisps)

1 Lay the slices of bread on a board and spread them evenly with butter. Turn the slices over, so the buttered sides are down, and spread the other sides with the mustard.

2 Layer the cheeses, tomato slices and bacon on four bread slices, overlapping or trimming the ingredients to fit. Top with the remaining bread, mustard sides down, and press gently to compress the sandwiches.

3 Heat a large, nonstick frying pan over medium heat. Working in batches, place the sandwiches in the pan and cook for about 3 minutes, pressing down gently and frequently until crisp and golden. Carefully turn and continue cooking for about 2 minutes longer, again pressing the sandwiches down until they are golden and the cheese is melting and beginning to ooze out. Repeat with the remaining sandwiches.

4 Transfer to a cutting board and slice in half. Serve immediately, with bread-and-butter pickle or chutney and potato chips.

29

Reuben Sandwich

There are various stories on the origins of this fried or grilled sandwich: it may take its name from a New York deli run by Arthur Reuben, who was said to have created the original sandwich for Annette Seelos, the lead in a 1914 Charlie Chaplin film. Alternatively, it may have been created by an Omaha grocer by the name of Reuben Kay who thought it up during a poker game. One of the poker player's employees won a sandwich competition with the idea a year later.

4 slices rye bread, with or without seeds
2 tbsp/25g butter, softened
4 tbsp Thousand Island dressing
4oz/115g corned beef (cooked salt beef),
   thinly sliced
½ cup/50g sauerkraut, well drained
1 cup/120g grated Swiss or Gruyère cheese
melted butter, for brushing

1 Butter one side of the rye bread and lay the slices, butter sides down, on a clean cutting board. Spread the other sides evenly with the Thousand Island dressing.

2 Cover 2 slices of bread with the corned beef, tucking in any long strips. Divide the sauerkraut and spread it in an even layer over the beef, then cover with the cheese. Top with the remaining bread slices, buttered side out, and press down to compress the sandwiches.

3 Heat a non-stick frying pan or griddle over medium-high heat, and cook the sandwiches, reducing the heat to medium, for about 4 minutes. Press the sandwiches gently with a metal spatula until they are golden. Carefully turn, and continue cooking until golden on the second side, about 2 minutes longer. Place on a cutting board, cut in half, and serve hot.

Chili Dogs

Serves 4–6

Whether he's a ball game fanatic or a couch potato, he'll be a fan of chili dogs. Along with hamburgers, they're the all-time favorite snack food. They're known by several nicknames, including 'hot dogs', after a cartoon depicting the frankfurter as such in a 1900s newspaper, as franks, or just plain dogs. These are hot dogs topped with chili made without the beans.

1 tbsp oil
4–6 good quality frankfurters or cooked bratwurst
4–6 frankfurter buns (hot dog rolls), split and warmed
2 cups/500ml homemade or bought chili without beans
1 onion, finely chopped

1 Heat the oil and 1 tablespoon water in a medium frying pan. Add the hot dogs and cook gently, turning frequently, until the water evaporates and the hot dogs are heated through and golden, about 10 minutes.

2 Meanwhile, heat the chili in a small saucepan over medium-low heat. Place a cooked frankfurter in each bun, and spoon the chili over it. Sprinkle with chopped onion, and serve in a folded paper napkin to catch the drips.

Bacon Cheeseburger with Red Onion Relish

Serves 4

When life was all fun and rock 'n' roll, the drive-in restaurant was the place to be for burgers, shakes and fries. With a cool car and smooth hair, all the guys made the most of the sunshine, sharing burgers with their girls in the parking lots. Live a little with these classic burgers and all the trimmings.

1¾ lb/800g ground (minced) beef
 (not too lean)
4–6 rindless bacon slices (rashers),
 cut in half
4 slices Monterey Jack or Cheddar cheese
4 sesame buns, split and toasted
lettuce leaves
sliced onion, mayonnaise, tomato ketchup,
 and pickles, to taste
salt and freshly ground black pepper
French fried potatoes, to serve

Red Onion Relish
2 tbsp vegetable oil
2 large red onions, coarsely chopped
1 small red chili, seeded and finely chopped
1 tbsp light brown sugar
½ tsp dried thyme
1–2 tbsp red wine vinegar
1–2 tsp butter
1–2 tbsp chopped fresh parsley

1 Prepare the relish first—it can be kept in the refrigerator for up to a week. Heat the oil in a heavy-based frying pan. Add the onions and chili, and cook for about 10 minutes, until softened, stirring frequently; do not allow to brown as the onions may become bitter.

2 Stir in the sugar, thyme, vinegar, and butter, and simmer for 10 minutes until the onions are soft and glazed. To prevent the mixture from scorching, add a little water. Remove from the heat and add the parsley. Cool, cover, and chill.

3 To make the burgers, gently break the beef

apart in a bowl, using a fork. Season with salt and pepper, and shape into 4 large patties. Chill until ready to cook.

4 Put the bacon slices in a heavy-based frying pan and cook over medium heat for about 6 minutes until crisp and browned, turning once. Drain on paper towel.

5 Pour off all but 2 tablespoons of the bacon fat and add the burgers to the pan. Cook until browned and juicy, turning once. Allow 6 minutes for rare or 7–8 minutes for a well-done burger. Just before the burgers are ready, top each with a slice of the cheese, and cook until the cheese begins to soften.

6 Arrange a lettuce leaf on the bottom of each bun, then place a burger on top. Add the bacon and a selection of condiments. Cover with the bun top and serve with the red onion relish and French fries.

Pigs in Blankets

No 1950s or '60s drinks bash would have been complete without these mini-sausage rolls and they remain as popular and delicious as ever. Men like them because they are satisfying and not too fancy. Serve them with a bowl of mustard for dipping.

1 tbsp/15g butter or oil
1 onion, finely chopped
12oz/350g good-quality sausage meat
1 tbsp dried mixed herbs, such as oregano,
    thyme, sage, tarragon and dill
12oz/350g bought puff pastry
a little freshly grated Parmesan cheese
1 egg, lightly beaten, for glazing
salt and freshly ground black
    pepper

1 In a small frying pan, heat the butter or oil over medium heat. Add the onion and cook for 3–4 minutes, until softened. Transfer to a mixing bowl and cool.

2 Add the sausage meat and herbs to the onion. Season with salt and pepper and stir until well blended.

3 Divide the mixture into four equal portions and roll into thin sausage shapes, each about 10in/25cm long. Roll the sausages on to a small baking sheet, cover and chill in the refrigerator or freezer until their edges are firm—this makes them easier to handle.

4 Preheat the oven to 425°F (220°C/Gas 7). Lightly grease 2 large baking sheets. On a lightly floured surface, roll out the puff pastry to about 1/8 in/3mm thick and cut into 4 strips, each measuring 10 x 3in/25 x 7.5cm. Place a chilled sausage on each strip and sprinkle with a little Parmesan cheese.

5 Brush one long edge of each pastry strip with beaten egg and roll up to enclose the sausage. Roll the long sausage rolls until their seam sides are down and press them gently to seal.

6 Cut each roll into 1in/2.5cm lengths and arrange these on the baking sheets. Brush each little roll with beaten egg and bake for about 15 minutes, until crisp and golden. Transfer to a wire rack to cool. Serve warm or at room temperature.

Deviled Eggs

Bring back fond memories of happy parties with these delicious little appetizers. They graced many a buffet table in the 1950s, '60s and '70s—and with good reason, as they are really tasty.

6 hard-cooked eggs
¼ cup/ 60g mayonnaise
1 tsp dry mustard
hot pepper sauce, to taste
24 capers, to garnish
salt and freshly ground black pepper

1 Tap each egg against a hard edge (such as a kitchen counter) to break the shell, then gently roll it on the surface to crack the whole shell evenly—this makes for easier peeling. Peel the eggs and cut them in half lengthwise.

2 Using a fork, scoop out the yolks into a small bowl. Mash the yolks against the side of the bowl and add the mayonnaise, mustard, salt and pepper, and hot pepper sauce to taste.

3 Using a small teaspoon, carefully pile the mixture into the whites. Alternatively, use a piping bag and tube to pipe the mixture into the whites. Top each egg with a caper. Place the eggs on a serving platter. Cover and chill until ready to serve.

Buttermilk Biscuits

He'll sniff the air appreciatively when you make a batch of these baking powder biscuits. The recipe uses vegetable shortening to produce tender, flaky little dinner rolls. They are popular on their own, with fried chicken or baked ham, or just about anything.

2 cups/225g all-purpose (plain) flour
1 tbsp baking powder
1 tbsp sugar (optional)
½ tsp salt
½ cup/120g white vegetable shortening
  (white vegetable fat), chilled
¾ cup/185ml buttermilk, chilled
melted butter, for brushing

1 Put the flour, baking powder, sugar (if using), and salt in a large mixing bowl and stir well to combine. Add the vegetable shortening and toss with the flour mixture. Using a pastry blender or your fingertips, rub in the shortening to form coarse crumbs.

2 Make a well in the middle and pour in the buttermilk. Using a fork, lightly stir in the flour to make a soft dough that begins to form a ball. Do not over mix—a few unblended pieces of fat will not matter. Turn out on to a lightly floured surface and knead gently five or six times, until the dough just holds together.

3 Lightly grease a large, heavy baking sheet. Preheat the oven to 450°F (230°C/Gas 8). Gently roll out the dough to a thickness of about ½in/1cm. Using a 2–2½in/5–6cm round cutter, cut out as many rounds as possible: press straight down and lift the cutter straight up without twisting. If you twist the cutter, the dough will be distorted and will rise unevenly. Place the dough rounds about 1½in/4cm apart on the baking sheet.

4 Gently knead the trimmings two or three times and pat or roll out, then stamp out rounds as before. Do not re-roll any further trimmings as they will be tough.

5 Bake for 10–12 minutes until risen, golden, and set. Brush each biscuit with a little melted butter and serve hot with extra cold butter.

Old-Fashioned Cornbread

Serves 6–8

Good, hearty man's food, this delicious Southern specialty is just yummy. If you prefer a smoother texture, use equal amounts of cornmeal and flour.

1/2 cup/120g butter, cut into cubes
1 1/4 cups/190g yellow cornmeal
3/4 cup/100g all-purpose (plain) flour
1/4 cup/55g sugar
1 tbsp baking powder
1/2 tsp salt
1 cup/250ml buttermilk
1 egg, lightly beaten
butter, to serve

1 Preheat the oven to 425°F (220°C/Gas 7). Put the butter in a 9–10in/23–25cm black iron frying pan or heavy ovenproof dish. Put in the oven for 3–5 minutes until the butter has melted. Swirl to coat the inside of the pan.

2 Meanwhile, put the cornmeal, flour, sugar, baking powder and salt in a large mixing bowl and stir to combine. Make a large well in the middle.

3 Set aside 2 tablespoons of the melted butter in a small bowl to cool slightly and pour the remainder into the middle of the dry ingredients. Keep the frying pan or dish warm. Using a fork, beat the egg and buttermilk together in a small bowl and beat in the reserved butter. Pour into the well in the cornmeal mixture and stir gently until just combined; do not over-mix. Pour the batter into the hot frying pan or dish.

4 Bake for 18–20 minutes until the cornbread top is set and golden and a cake tester or metal skewer comes out with just a few crumbs attached when inserted into the middle. Serve hot or warm, with butter.

Popovers

Make him a batch of these incredibly light batter rolls to mop up the juices from his steak. They were very popular in the 1960s and '70s and were served in most steak houses as an accompaniment. Beating the batter until it is very airy makes them rise.

Makes 8

6 tbsp/90g butter, melted
6 eggs
2 cups/500ml milk
2 cups/225g all-purpose (plain) flour
1 tsp salt
butter, for serving

1 Preheat the oven to 375°F (190°C/Gas 5). Use some of the melted butter to grease eight deep custard cups (about 1 scant cup/225ml), or deep muffin pan cups generously. If using custard cups, set them on a baking sheet for easier handling. Set aside.

2 Use an electric beater to beat the eggs in a large bowl for 2–3 minutes, until frothy. Beat in the milk and remaining butter until blended, then beat in the flour and salt to make a smooth batter.

3 Using a ladle, carefully fill each custard cup or muffin pan cup three-quarters full. Bake for about 1 hour. Quickly pierce the popovers near the top to allow some steam to escape and continue baking for 10 minutes longer. Remove from the cups and serve immediately, with extra butter.

what's for supper darling?

When he comes in through the front door feeling
half starved and ready to eat you out of house and
home, give him a big kiss, sit him down at the
table, and serve him up one of these delicious supper
dishes. A bowl of fragrant soup will gently soothe his
frazzled spirits—he'll adore a robust Black Bean Soup,
or a classic Chicken Noodle Soup with Vegetables. After
a long day at work, he needs something tasty and
satisfying—so next time he yells "What's for supper,
darling?" combat those growls of hunger with tough guy
suppers of Corned Beef Hash and Eggs, Franks and Beans
and Baked Macaroni and Cheese. That should keep him
quiet for a while!

Chicken Noodle Soup with Vegetables

Soothe his weary spirits with this hearty soup. It will take him back to the security of childhood, when his mother banished winter chills with this warming favorite. Ever popular, this delicious dish was found on most 1950s diner menus.

8 cups/2lt chicken stock
   (preferably homemade)
1 large onion, finely chopped
3 carrots, halved lengthwise and
   thinly sliced
2 celery stalks, thinly sliced
2 small zucchini (courgettes),
   thinly sliced (optional)
4oz/115g thin egg noodles (vermicelli)
   or other pasta
1 cup/180g shredded or diced cooked
   chicken
2 tbsp finely chopped parsley
salt and freshly ground black pepper
saltine crackers or water biscuits,
   to serve (optional)

1 Pour the chicken stock into a large saucepan or Dutch oven (flameproof casserole) and bring to a boil over medium-high heat. Skim off any fat or foam that rises to the surface, then reduce the heat to medium.

2 Add the onion, carrots, and celery, and simmer for about 10 minutes, until the vegetables are just tender. Stir in the zucchini and cook for a further 3 minutes.

3 Add the noodles to the simmering soup and cook for 3–4 minutes or according to the directions on the package.

4 When the noodles are tender, stir in the cooked chicken and parsley, season with salt and pepper, and heat through. Serve steaming hot with saltine crackers or water biscuits (if using).

COOK'S TIP

Instead of using noodles, you can use the same quantity of rice. Also, if you prefer a clear, thin broth, cook the noodles or rice separately, then drain and rinse them before adding to the soup.

Black Bean Soup

Serves 4–6

He'll love the earthy flavor of black beans; they are frequently used in Creole and Caribbean cookery.
This thick and hearty soup was made famous by The Coach House restaurant in New York City.

1 lb/450g dried black beans, soaked
  overnight
2 celery stalks, diced
1 large onion, chopped
1 large carrot, diced
1 garlic clove, finely chopped
1 bay leaf
salt and freshly ground black pepper
dry sherry (optional), to serve
2 hard-cooked eggs, chopped, to garnish

Ham Stock

1–2 large meaty ham bones
2 large onions, peeled but left whole
2 celery stalks, roughly chopped
2 large carrots, cut into chunks
4 cloves
12 black peppercorns
2 bay leaves
2 garlic cloves

1 To prepare the stock, trim the meat from the bones and cut into bite-sized pieces. Place the meat in a bowl, cover and chill. Put the bones, onions, celery, and carrots in a stockpot or large, deep saucepan. Cover with cold water and bring to a boil over medium-high heat.

2 Skim off any foam that rises to the surface. Reduce the heat and add the cloves, peppercorns, bay leaves, and garlic. Simmer for at least 2 hours, skimming off any surface residue occasionally. Strain the stock into a large bowl or saucepan; discard the bones and vegetables.

3 Drain the black beans and put them in a Dutch oven (flameproof casserole) or large saucepan. Cover with fresh cold water and bring to a boil over high heat. Boil hard for about 5 minutes, drain, rinse, and return to the Dutch oven or pan.

4 Add about 8 cups/2lt of the stock, the celery, onion, carrot, garlic, and bay leaf. Bring to a boil, reduce the heat to low and simmer for about 2 hours, stirring occasionally, until the beans and vegetables are very tender.

5 Remove the bay leaf. Using a potato masher or slotted spoon, mash the beans slightly to give the soup a chunky texture. Add the reserved ham and heat through. Add salt and pepper to taste and extra stock or water if the soup is too thick.

6 To serve, ladle the soup into large bowls. Stir a little sherry into each portion (if using) and garnish with chopped hard-cooked egg.

Chop Suey

Hand him the chopsticks! He'll love this—it's a tasty dish originally introduced by Chinese immigrants who were the trail cooks during the building of the Pacific Railroad in the 1860s. In China there's no such dish as chop suey; it's named after 'tsa sui', the Mandarin words for chopped odds and ends. This sounded like 'chop suey' to the Western workers.

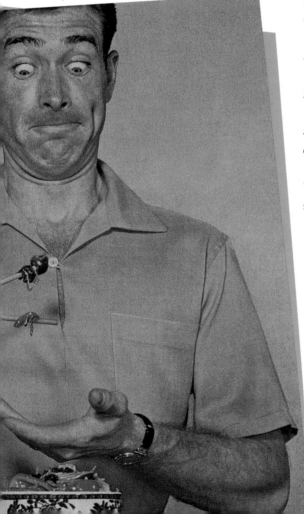

2 tbsp cornstarch (cornflour)

3 tbsp soy sauce

1 tbsp dry sherry

1in/2.5cm piece fresh ginger root, grated or finely chopped

1/2 cup/125ml water

2 tbsp vegetable oil

1lb/450g pork tenderloin or skinless, boneless chicken breast, cut into thin strips

1 small head Chinese cabbage, finely shredded

2–3 celery stalks, finely sliced on the diagonal into 1/2in/1cm pieces

6–8 green (spring) onions, sliced on the diagonal into 1/2in/1cm pieces

1lb/450g bean sprouts, rinsed

6–81/2 oz/175–240g can water chestnuts, drained and sliced

5–6oz/150–175g can bamboo shoots, drained and sliced

2 tbsp chopped cilantro (coriander leaves) or parsley

salt and freshly ground black pepper

cooked rice, to serve

1 In a small bowl, combine the cornstarch, soy sauce, sherry, salt and pepper, ginger and water until well blended; set aside.

2 Heat the oil over medium-high heat in a wok or large heavy based frying pan. Add the pork or chicken and stir-fry for about 4 minutes. Stir the cornstarch mixture and stir it into the pork—the mixture will thicken as it comes to the boil.

3 Add the cabbage, celery, green onions, bean sprouts, water chestnuts, bamboo shoots and cilantro, and stir-fry for about 5 minutes longer, until the meat is cooked and vegetables are just tender. Serve on rice.

Buffalo-Style Chicken Wings with Blue Cheese Dip

Makes 48

Wake up his taste buds with these fiery chicken wings. They were an immediate hit when they were first served at the Anchor Bar in Buffalo, New York, in 1964. The hot sauce makes a great barbecue marinade for other chicken pieces, too.

24 plump chicken wings, tips removed
vegetable oil, for frying
celery stalks, to serve

Blue Cheese Dip

4oz/115g blue cheese, such as Danish Blue
1/2 cup/115g mayonnaise
1/2 cup/125g sour cream
2–3 green (spring) onions, finely chopped
1 garlic clove, crushed
1 tbsp white wine vinegar

Hot Pepper Sauce

4 tbsp/55g butter
1/2 tsp salt
1/4 cup/60ml hot pepper or chile sauce
1 tbsp white wine vinegar
cayenne pepper, to taste

COOK'S TIP

Alternatively, you can marinate the chicken wings in the sauce and barbecue or broil (grill) them. Prepare the hot pepper sauce and leave it to cool to room temperature. Place the wings in a bowl and pour over the sauce, then cover and leave to marinate for 20–25 minutes. Broil (grill) the wings under medium heat for 20–25 minutes, turning once halfway through cooking and basting frequently with the sauce. Cool slightly before serving with the dip.

1 Make the dip before cooking the chicken wings: using a fork, roughly mash the blue cheese. Stir in the mayonnaise, sour cream, green onions, garlic and wine vinegar, until blended—the dip should not be completely smooth. Chill until ready to serve.

2 Using kitchen scissors or a heavy knife, cut each chicken wing in half at the joint to make 48 pieces. Heat about 2in/5cm depth of oil in a wok or large saucepan until hot, but not smoking. Working in small batches, fry a few wing pieces at a time for about 10 minutes, until crisp and golden, turning once. Drain on paper towels and arrange in a heatproof bowl.

3 For the hot pepper sauce, melt the butter in a small saucepan over medium-low heat. Stir in the salt, hot pepper or chile sauce, vinegar and a pinch or 'knife tip' of cayenne pepper. Stir to combine the ingredients and cook for 10–15 seconds.

4 Pour the sauce over the fried wings and toss to coat all the pieces. Serve immediately, with the dip and celery.

Corned Beef Hash and Eggs

Serves 4

Men adore this dish! It was so popular at the turn of the nineteenth century that the places that served it were called 'hash houses' and the cooks 'hash slingers'. At home, this was the best way to use Sunday's leftover meat and roast potatoes for Monday's supper. The egg made it a more substantial meal.

4 tbsp/55g butter or oil
1 large onion, chopped
2½lb/1.25kg cooked potatoes, diced
3 cups/500g cooked corned beef
  (salt beef), diced
½ cup/125ml heavy (double) cream
2–3 tbsp chopped parsley
1 tsp Worcestershire sauce
pinch of cayenne pepper
4 extra large, very fresh eggs
salt and freshly ground black pepper

1 Heat the butter or oil in a large nonstick frying pan over medium heat. Add the onion and cook for about 5 minutes until softened and just beginning to brown.

2 Stir in the potatoes, beef, cream, and half the parsley. Season with Worcestershire sauce, cayenne pepper, and salt and pepper.

3 Spread the mixture evenly and flatten the hash to form a slight crust on the bottom. Cook for about 10 minutes, until beginning to brown. Run the spatula around the edge of the pan occasionally to prevent the mixture from sticking. Turn the hash to break it up and continue cooking until it is crisp and well browned.

4 Use a spoon to make four deep indentations in the hash and break the eggs into the indentations. Reduce the heat to low and cook, covered, for about 10 minutes or until the eggs are set. Garnish with the remaining chopped parsley and serve from the pan.

red flannel hash

hash pie

Easy Burritos

Serves 4-6 Get him into an easy going, Tex-Mex mood with this tasty dish. It has always been a favorite in Texas and other south-western states, but by the late 1950s it was so popular that people were cooking it at home. Burritos are fun for a casual, serve-yourself supper party—put out all the fillings and accompaniments and let each guest assemble their own filled tortilla.

4–6 large flour tortillas
2–3 tbsp vegetable oil
1 onion, coarsely chopped
1 red or green bell pepper, seeded
  and chopped
1 garlic clove, crushed
1¹/₂lb/675g boneless pork loin or skinless
  boneless chicken breast, thinly sliced
¹/₂ tsp crushed chilies, or to taste
¹/₂ tsp ground cumin
11oz/300g can sweet corn kernels, drained
2 ripe tomatoes, chopped
salt and freshly ground black pepper

To Serve
any or all of the following: bottled taco
  sauce, sliced avocado, sliced red onion,
  shredded iceberg lettuce, grated Monterey
  Jack or Cheddar cheese, sour cream,
  chopped cilantro (fresh coriander leaves)

1 Preheat the oven to 350°F (180°C/Gas 4). Wrap the tortillas tightly in aluminum foil and heat in the oven for about 15 minutes.

2 Meanwhile, in a large frying pan or wok, heat 2 tablespoons of oil over medium-high heat, add the onion, pepper, and garlic and stir-fry 2–3 minutes, until beginning to soften. Transfer to a plate and set aside.

3 Add the remaining oil and the pork or chicken, crushed chilies, and cumin, and stir fry for about 3 minutes. Season with salt and pepper and return the cooked vegetables to the pan. Add the sweet corn and tomatoes, and cook 2–3 minutes longer until heated through.

4 Lay the warm tortillas on a surface and divide the mixture evenly among them, placing it near one edge. Top with the chosen accompaniments. Fold the edge nearest the filling over just enough to cover the filling. Fold the two sides over to form an envelope shape. Serve with extra taco sauce, if you like.

Franks and Beans

This universally popular supper dish can be mocked up in 2 minutes in the microwave using the famous Heinz Baked Beans. But he deserves the real thing, so give him a real taste treat, and make your own Boston baked beans. He'll know the difference right away.

Serves 6-8

2 cups/500g dried navy (haricot) beans, soaked overnight
6 cups/1.5lt cold water
1/4 cup/60ml dark molasses
2 tbsp packed light brown sugar or maple syrup
1 tbsp dry mustard
1 tbsp Worcestershire sauce
2/3 cup/150ml tomato sauce, chopped tomatoes or tomato ketchup
1 cup/250ml water
1 red onion, studded with 6–8 whole cloves
4oz/115g piece of salt pork or thick bacon
6–8 frankfurters
salt and freshly ground black pepper

1 Drain and rinse the soaked beans. Place them in a large heavy saucepan or Dutch oven (flameproof casserole) and cover with the water. Bring to a boil over high heat, skimming off any foam that rises to the surface. Boil hard for 3 minutes, reduce the heat to low and simmer, covered, for about 1 1/2 hours or until tender.

2 Preheat the oven to 350°F (180°C/Gas 4). Drain the beans, reserving the cooking liquid. In a 2 1/2 quart/2.5lt bean pot or casserole, combine the molasses, brown sugar or maple syrup, mustard, Worcestershire sauce and tomato sauce, tomatoes or ketchup with the water, stirring to blend well. Pour in 1 cup/250ml of the reserved bean cooking liquid and add the beans, stirring gently.

3 Push the clove-studded onion into the middle of the beans. Score the salt pork or bacon at 1in/2.5cm intervals on the rind side and place on top of the beans, pushing it into the beans gently so all but the rind is submerged. Bake for about 3 hours, adding a little more of the reserved bean liquid, if necessary, to keep the ingredients covered. Uncover the pot for the final 30 minutes of cooking to allow the pork rind to crisp.

4 Meanwhile, bring a saucepan half-filled with water to a boil over medium heat. Carefully drop in the frankfurters and simmer for 2–3 minutes; alternatively, follow the directions on the package. Drain the frankfurters.

5 Remove the salt pork and onion from the beans. Cut the frankfurters into small dice, stir them into the beans and serve.

Baked Macaroni and Cheese

The aroma, flavor and texture of this classic supper dish epitomizes all that is good about Mama's home cooking—and it brings a warm glow to every man's heart as well as to his stomach.

1lb/450g macaroni
4 tbsp/55g butter, plus extra for 'dotting'
1 large onion, finely chopped
1/3 cup/75g all-purpose (plain) flour
4 cups/1lt milk
1 bay leaf
1/2 tsp dried thyme
1/2 tsp cayenne pepper
1 tsp mustard powder
2 small leeks, finely chopped, blanched and
   drained
3oz/75g cooked ham, diced
1lb/450g sharp Cheddar cheese, grated
2 tbsp dried natural bread crumbs
2 tbsp grated Parmesan cheese
salt and freshly ground black pepper

1 Preheat the oven to 350°F (180°C/Gas 4) and lightly grease a 13 x 9in/33 x 23cm baking dish. Bring a large pan of salted water to a boil. Stir in the macaroni and cook for about 10 minutes, until al dente. Drain and rinse under cold water; set aside.

2 In a heavy-based saucepan, melt the butter over medium-low heat. Add the onion and cook until soft and translucent, stirring frequently. Sprinkle over the flour and stir until well blended. Cook for 2–3 minutes.

3 Whisk in a quarter of the milk, then gradually whisk in the remaining milk. Add the thyme, season with salt, and simmer until thick and smooth, about 15 minutes. Season with the black pepper, cayenne, and mustard powder.

4 Remove the sauce from the heat and stir in the drained leeks, ham, and all but a handful of the grated Cheddar cheese. When the cheese has melted and is well blended stir in the cooked macaroni. Transfer to the baking dish and spread out evenly. Place the dish on a large baking sheet.

5 Sprinkle the remaining Cheddar cheese over the macaroni. Combine the bread crumbs and Parmesan, and sprinkle on top. Dot with butter and bake for about 30 minutes, until well browned and crisp. Serve piping hot.

Western Omelet

Makes 2

Bring out his rugged pioneer side with a Western omelet— they're always a popular choice in diners, roadside cafés and 'greasy spoons' everywhere, and are usually accompanied by French fries or hash brown potatoes.

3 tbsp/45g butter
1 small onion, finely chopped
1/2 green bell pepper, seeded
  and diced
2oz/50g cooked ham, diced
4–6 eggs

parsley sprigs, to garnish
salt and freshly ground black pepper
buttered toast, to serve (optional)

Eggs Benedict

Serves 4

He'll be full of empathy when you tell him this story. It is said that this classic egg dish was created by the chef at the Waldorf Hotel for a regular customer, Mr Benedict, who was suffering with a hangover. True or not, this elegant dish remains a popular choice for a light supper, Sunday breakfast or brunch.

4 thick rindless Canadian-style (back)
  bacon slices (rashers)
1 tbsp white wine vinegar
4 extra large, very fresh eggs
2 English muffins, split, toasted and
  buttered
watercress sprigs, to garnish

Easy Hollandaise Sauce
3 egg yolks
2 tbsp freshly squeezed lemon juice
1/2 tsp salt
pinch of cayenne pepper
1/2 cup/120g butter
2 tbsp light (single) cream

1 Prepare the easy Hollandaise sauce first: put the egg yolks and lemon juice in a food processor or blender. Season with salt and cayenne pepper to taste. Process for 15 seconds to blend.

2 Melt the butter in a small saucepan over medium heat until bubbling and skim off any foam. With the motor running, pour the hot butter into the food processor or blender in a thin, steady stream—do not pour in the milky solids at the bottom of the pan.

3 Process for a few seconds until the sauce is well blended. Add the cream and pulse until blended.

1 Heat 1 tablespoon of the butter in a nonstick frying pan over medium heat. Add the onion and green pepper and cook, stirring often, until just beginning to soften. Stir in the ham and season with salt and pepper. Transfer the mixture to a large plate and keep warm.

2 Beat the eggs until well blended and season with salt and pepper. Melt half the remaining butter in the pan and increase the heat to medium-high. When the foam subsides, pour in half the beaten egg mixture.

3 Use a fork to lift the edges of the omelet, tilting the pan so the uncooked egg runs underneath. Shake the pan sharply back and fore over the heat so that the omelet slides freely.

4 When the egg is lightly cooked, but still creamy, spoon half the vegetable mixture over half the omelet. Using a spatula, lift and fold the uncovered half over the filling. Carefully slide the omelet on to a warm plate.

5 Repeat with the remaining butter, egg mixture, and vegetable mixture. Garnish the omelets with parsley and arrange toast triangles around them (if serving). Serve immediately.

Scrape the sauce into a heatproof bowl and keep warm over hot water.

4 In a large frying pan, cook the bacon over medium heat for 5–6 minutes, turning once. Remove from the heat and keep warm.

5 Meanwhile, in another large frying pan, bring about 1 inch/2.5cm depth of water to a boil. Stir in the vinegar. Break an egg into a cup. Using a wooden spoon, stir the water in a corner of the pan to create a swirl or vortex, then gently slide the egg into the middle. Repeat with the remaining eggs.

6 Reduce the heat and simmer for 3–4 minutes until the eggs are lightly cooked or set to your taste. Using a slotted spoon, transfer the eggs to a plate lined with paper towel to drain. Trim off any ragged edges of egg white.

7 Arrange a slice of bacon on each buttered muffin half, trimming the meat to fit, and top with a poached egg. Spoon a little warm sauce over the eggs, garnish each with a sprig of watercress and serve.

Cheese Fondue

If your man is a lover of cheese he'll certainly adore this dish. It originated in Switzerland, where the locals devised this one-pot dish to use up any leftover pieces of hard cheese.

Cheese fondue became popular in the 1950s as 'après ski' fare, and by the 1960s it was one of the most popular party foods. The obligatory fondue pot appeared on every girl's wedding list.

3 garlic cloves, bruised
2½ cups/600ml dry white wine
1½lb/675g grated Gruyère or Emmental cheese
3 tbsp arrowroot or all-purpose (plain) flour
3 tbsp/45g butter
freshly grated nutmeg
¼ cup/60ml whipping cream
3 tbsp kirsch
salt and freshly ground white pepper

To Serve
French bread, cut into cubes and lightly toasted
selection of crisp or firm vegetables, such as chunks of celery, radishes, cauliflower florets, and boiled small new potatoes
green salad (optional)

1 Bring the garlic and white wine to a boil in a medium, heavy-based saucepan. Boil until reduced by about a quarter. Remove and discard the garlic cloves and reduce the heat to low.

2 In a bowl, toss the cheese with the arrowroot or flour. Add half the butter to the wine and begin adding the cheese a little at a time, stirring with a wooden fork or spoon until each addition has completely melted before adding more. When all the cheese has been added, season with salt, pepper and freshly grated nutmeg to taste.

3 Add the remaining butter and half the cream and continue to cook for 2–3 minutes, until the mixture thickens to resemble thick custard in texture. Add the remaining cream and then stir in the kirsch.

4 Pour the fondue into a warm fondue pot and set over its burner. Serve with the bread and vegetables. Provide long-handled fondue forks to spear and dunk pieces of bread or vegetable into the fondue. Using a twisting motion to remove the food from the melted cheese catches the delicious drips. Offer a green salad with the fondue, if you like.

COOK'S TIP
If the fondue becomes too thick, stir in a little more cream or white wine. Control the heat from the burner to prevent the fondue from burning. The golden crust that forms on the bottom of the pan is the gourmet treat to be shared out when the creamy dip is finished.

rib-stickin' good meals

For those times when nothing less than hearty home cooking will do, bring back good old-fashioned "Wow!" into eating. These are the dishes that made men feel great and gave their women those wonderful satisfied, smug smiles. Cut into Deep-Dish Chicken Pot Pie at the table and smell the first burst of steaming hot goodness escaping the crust. Go retro by serving crunchy Southern-Fried Chicken with Cornsticks in napkin-lined baskets or make no-fuss Beef Stew with Herb Dumplings for an irresistible meal.

Southern-Fried Chicken with Cornsticks

Serves 6

Traditional Southern-fried chicken is a big hit with most guys, and most experienced cooks have a pet recipe—the big debate is whether to soak the chicken in buttermilk for super-succulent results that contrast with the crunchy coating. Cornsticks baked in pans shaped like corn-cobs are the classic and delicious accompaniment.

1½ cups/375ml buttermilk
2 tsp salt
cayenne pepper
freshly ground black pepper
8 skinless, boneless chicken breast halves
  or other pieces
1½ cups/175g all-purpose (plain) flour
vegetable oil, for frying

Cornsticks

1 cup/120g all-purpose (plain) flour
¾ cup/75g fine or medium cornmeal
2 tbsp sugar
1 tbsp baking powder
1 tsp salt
1 egg
⅔ cup/150ml milk
⅓ cup/75g butter or margarine,
  melted and cooled

1 In a shallow dish, combine the buttermilk, half the salt, ½ teaspoon cayenne pepper, and black pepper to taste. Add the chicken and coat each piece evenly. Cover and chill for at least 2 hours or up to 24 hours, turning once.

2 To prepare the cornsticks, preheat the oven to 425°F (220°C/Gas 7). Grease 14 cornstick cups. Combine the flour, cornmeal, sugar, baking powder, and salt in a bowl and make a well in the middle. Whisk the egg, milk, and butter or margarine until blended; pour into the flour mixture and stir to mix.

3 Spoon the batter into the cups, filling each three-quarters full. Bake for 15 minutes until puffed and golden. Cool for 2–3 minutes before removing the cornsticks from their cups. Repeat with the remaining batter, regreasing the cups. Serve the cornsticks warm.

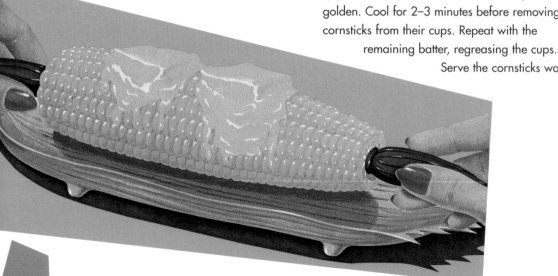

4 Meanwhile, drain and cook the chicken: put the flour in a plastic bag and add the remaining salt with cayenne pepper and black pepper to taste. Close the bag and shake to mix. Drop 2 or 3 pieces of the drained chicken into the bag, and shake gently to coat evenly. Shake off any excess flour and place the pieces on a wire rack. Repeat with the remaining pieces.

5 Heat ¹/₂in/1cm depth of oil in a deep frying pan to 350°F/180°C. Carefully lower the chicken pieces into the hot oil, skin-side down. Cook, turning once, until crisp and golden all over, about 10 minutes. Drain well. Serve hot with the cornsticks.

COOK'S TIP
If you do not have decorative cornstick cups, the batter can be baked in a regular muffin pan.

Chicken Kiev

This makes a great, finger-licking treat and always goes down well with hungry males. During the 1960s and '70s these boned chicken breasts filled with garlic butter were all the rage in restaurants and at home.

1/2 cup/120g butter, softened
1 tbsp lemon juice
1 garlic clove, mashed with a little salt
1 tbsp finely chopped parsley
4 large part-boned chicken breasts, with
  wings attached, skinned
1/3 cup/75g all-purpose (plain) flour
2 eggs
1 1/2 cups/75g fresh white bread crumbs
vegetable oil, for deep-frying
salt and freshly ground black pepper
parsley sprigs, to garnish

1 In a small bowl, cream the butter, lemon juice, garlic, and parsley until well blended. Chill until beginning to firm up—about 20 minutes.

2 Place each chicken breast between plastic wrap (cling film) and gently roll the meat with a rolling pin to flatten it without making any holes in it. Turn the breasts with the wings down and season with salt and pepper.

3 Scrape the butter on to a piece of plastic wrap (cling film) and, using the wrap as a guide, roll the butter into a thin sausage shape. Cut into 4 pieces and lay a piece on each chicken breast.

4 Starting at the far end, roll up the chicken fillet around the butter towards the wing joint, tucking in the sides. The bone will act as a handle. Be sure the butter is completely enclosed.

5 Put the flour in a plastic bag and put a chicken breast in the bag. Twist the bag to close the end and roll the chicken gently to coat it completely in flour. Repeat with the remaining chicken.

6 Beat the eggs in a shallow bowl and put the bread crumbs in another bowl. Dip a piece of floured chicken in the egg, turning to coat the entire portion, then into the bread crumbs, rolling to coat it completely. Repeat with the remaining chicken, egg and bread crumbs. Arrange on a plate, cover and chill for at least 2 hours or overnight.

7 Heat the oil for deep-frying to 365°F/185°C or until a small cube of day-old bread browns in about 60 seconds. Add the chicken pieces and fry gently for about 5 minutes, turning once, until crisp and golden. Drain well on paper towels and serve immediately, garnished with parsley.

COOK'S TIP

If necessary, to part-bone chicken breast quarters, using a small sharp knife, cut off the first 2 joints of the chicken wing (reserve these for another use). Remove the skin and carefully bone the breasts by sliding the knife between the breast bone and the flesh, keeping the knife against the ribs and leaving the last wing joint attached to the breast meat (reserve the rib cage for another use).

Chicken Hunter-style

When your man comes in from the great outdoors, all tuckered out after a day's hunting, serve him up a tasty meal of chicken cooked 'hunter-style'—it has been a popular supper dish at home since the 1950s and is still a great way of using chicken pieces.

1/2 cup/50g all-purpose (plain) flour
2 1/2 lb/1.25kg chicken portions
3-4 tbsp vegetable oil
1 onion, sliced
1lb/450g mushrooms, sliced
1 garlic clove, crushed
1/4 cup/60ml dry white wine
1/2 cup/125ml chicken stock or water
14 1/2 oz/415g can chopped tomatoes
1 tbsp chopped oregano
1 1/2 tsp chopped thyme
sprigs oregano or thyme to garnish
salt and freshly ground black pepper
boiled spaghetti, to serve

1 Put the flour in a plastic bag and season with salt and pepper; shake to mix. Drop the chicken portions into the bag, one at a time, and shake to coat with the flour. Gently tap off any excess and put the floured chicken on a plate.

2 Heat the oil in a Dutch oven (flameproof casserole) over medium-high heat. Add the chicken and cook until golden on all sides, turning as necessary. Transfer to a plate.

3 Add the onions and mushrooms to the oil remaining in the pan, adding a little more if necessary, and cook, stirring frequently, for about 7 minutes until golden. Add the garlic and cook for a further 20–30 seconds.

4 Pour in the wine and stir to scrape up any cooking residue on the pan, then add the stock or water and the tomatoes. Season with salt and pepper and replace the chicken with any juices that have seeped from it.

5 Bring to the boil, reduce the heat to low and cover the pan. Simmer for about 40 minutes, until the chicken is tender and cooked through and the juices are thickened. Baste the chicken occasionally, if necessary, during cooking.

6 Tilt the pan to skim off any excess fat, then stir in the herbs. Serve with boiled spaghetti and garnish with oregano or thyme sprigs.

COOK'S TIP

The wine can be omitted and an additional 1/4 cup/60ml stock or water added instead. Dried herbs can be used instead of fresh: add 1 teaspoon dried oregano or 1/2 teaspoon dried thyme in step 4, with the tomatoes.

Deep-Dish Chicken Pot Pie

Serves 6–8 Men love home-baked pies, and this traditional dish will really stick to his ribs. The original pot pie was baked in a deep pot, hence the name, and the first commercial frozen version was a chicken pie made by Swanson in 1951. It's an ideal way to use up leftover cooked chicken or turkey.

2 cups/ 225g all-purpose (plain) flour
1 tsp salt
¼ cup/ 60g butter, cut into pieces
½ cup/ 120g white vegetable shortening (white vegetable fat), cut into pieces
about 4 tbsp ice water
1 egg, lightly beaten, to glaze

Creamy Chicken Filling
2½ cups/ 600ml chicken stock (preferably homemade)
2lb/ 900g skinless, boneless chicken breasts
3–4 carrots, cut into 1in/ 2.5cm pieces
3 celery stalks, thickly sliced
10oz/ 275g pearl onions, peeled
1 cup/ 155g frozen peas
6 tbsp/ 90g butter
½ cup/ 55g all-purpose (plain) flour
1 cup/ 250ml heavy (double) cream
1 tsp chopped thyme or ½ tsp dried thyme
2–3 tbsp snipped chives
3 tbsp chopped parsley
salt and freshly ground black pepper

1 To make the pastry, put the flour and salt into the bowl of a food processor and pulse to mix. Add the butter and shortening and process until the mixture forms coarse crumbs. With the machine running, add the water a tablespoon at a time until the mixture forms a dough: do not allow the dough to form into a ball around the blade or the pastry will be tough. When the dough begins to stick together, turn it out on to a piece of plastic wrap (cling film) and use the wrap to shape the dough into a ball, then flatten it. Wrap and chill for at least 1 hour.

2 Meanwhile, make the filling. Bring the chicken stock to a boil in a large saucepan over medium-high heat. Add the chicken breasts, reduce the heat to medium and simmer until just cooked, about 15 minutes. Remove from the heat and cool the chicken in the broth. Lift the chicken from the stock when cool, cut it into chunks and set aside.

3 Bring the stock to a boil. Add the carrots and cook over high heat for about 5 minutes until the carrots are par-cooked. Add the celery and pearl onions and cook about 3 minutes longer, then add the peas. Strain the stock and set aside the vegetables. Measure 2½ cups/600ml stock and set aside.

4 In a heavy-based saucepan, melt the butter over medium heat. Whisk in the flour and cook for 2–3 minutes until bubbling and smooth. Gradually whisk in the measured stock and bring to a boil. Reduce the heat to medium and simmer for about 5 minutes, until smooth and thick. Stir in the cream and cook for a further 5 minutes.

5 Add the thyme, chives and parsley to the sauce and season with salt and pepper. Stir in the vegetables and chicken and pour into a 9 x13in/ 23 x 33cm deep baking dish. Spread the filling evenly, then set aside to cool.

6 Preheat the oven to 400°F (200°C/Gas 6). On a lightly floured surface, roll out the pastry to about 1/8in/3mm thick. Brush the edge of the dish with beaten egg. Trim the pastry to about 1in/2.5cm larger than the dish and lift it over the filling. Fold the overhanging pastry under and press it into a stand-up edge. Crimp the edges by pinching them between your fingers.

7 Brush the pie with beaten egg. Use a sharp knife to make 2–3 slits in the top to allow steam to escape. If you like, cut out leaves or other decorations from the pastry trimmings, press them gently on the pie and glaze again.

8 Place the pie in the oven and immediately reduce the temperature to 350°F (180°C/Gas 5). Bake for about 35 minutes, until the pastry is golden brown and the mixture bubbling. Let the pie stand a few minutes before serving.

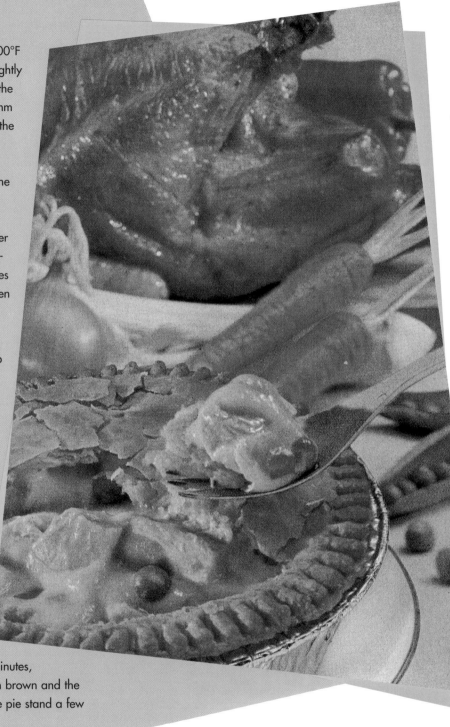

Roast Turkey with Sausage and Sage Stuffing

Serves 10–12

Hand him the carving tools for his great 'big daddy' moment at the table! Roast turkey is the main attraction at many festive dinners, especially Thanksgiving and Christmas when the family gathers together. This superb bird is usually served with all the trimmings—cranberry sauce, sweet potatoes, stuffing, and, of course, gravy.

12–14lb/4.5–5.5kg turkey with giblets, neck, and wing tips removed for gravy
1 cup/225g butter, softened
1/2 tsp dried thyme
1/2 tsp dried sage
2 cups/500ml chicken or turkey stock
watercress or herb sprigs, to garnish

Sausage and Sage Stuffing
2 tbsp/25g butter
1 onion, chopped
2–3 celery stalks, thinly sliced
1lb/450g sausage meat
2 garlic cloves, crushed
2 tbsp chopped sage or 1 tbsp dried sage
1 tbsp dried thyme
1 cup/120g pecan nuts, toasted and chopped (optional)
1lb/450g firm-textured white bread, crusts removed, cut into small cubes
2–3 cups/500–750ml chicken or turkey stock, preferably homemade
2 eggs, lightly beaten
salt and freshly ground black pepper

Giblet Gravy
turkey neck, giblets, and wing tips
1 onion, chopped
2 celery stalks, chopped
12 parsley stems
2 bay leaves
3–4 thyme sprigs
1 tsp black peppercorns
4 tbsp all-purpose (plain) flour

1 To prepare the stuffing, melt the butter in a large saucepan. Add the onion and celery and cook, stirring frequently, for about 4 minutes, until the vegetables begin to soften. Add the sausage meat and garlic and cook, stirring to break up the meat, for about 4 minutes, until the meat is no longer pink. Stir in the sage, thyme, and pecans, if using, and remove from the heat.

2 Add the bread to the stuffing and toss to combine it with the other ingredients. Stir in half the stock and season with salt and pepper. Add more stock if the mixture seems dry, then cool slightly.

3 Stir the beaten eggs into the stuffing adding a little more stock, if necessary, so that the stuffing holds together but is not too wet. Set aside the stuffing. (This can be prepared a day ahead, covered and chilled.)

4 Put all the ingredients for the giblet gravy except the flour in a large saucepan or stockpot and pour in at least 6 cups/1.5lt cold water or enough to

cover the ingredients. Bring to the boil over high heat, skimming any foam that rises to the surface. Reduce the heat to low and simmer, partially covered, for about 2 hours, adding more water if necessary.

5 Strain the giblet stock into a large bowl. If you like, chop the cooked giblets and neck meat and reserve them to add to the gravy. When the stock is cold, skim any fat from the surface and chill. (The stock can be made up to 2 days in advance.)

6 To prepare the turkey, preheat the oven to 325°F (160°C/Gas 3). Rinse the turkey cavity and dry with paper towels, then season with salt and pepper. In a small bowl, cream the butter with the thyme, sage, and salt and pepper. Using your fingertips and starting with the neck end, separate the skin from the meat on both sides of the breast. Spread half the butter under the skin, pushing it as far under the skin as possible. Rub the remaining butter over the whole turkey. Tuck the neck skin under the bird and secure it closed with a skewer.

7 Spoon the stuffing into the cavity and secure the opening with skewers. Tie the legs together with string. Alternatively, stuff the neck end before tucking the skin under and securing it. Place any leftover stuffing in a greased baking dish and cover with foil: this can be baked in the oven with the turkey for about 1 hour at the end of cooking.

8 Set the turkey on a rack in a roasting pan and pour about 1 cup/250ml of the stock into the pan. Roast the turkey for 3½–4½ hours or until a meat thermometer inserted into the thickest part of the thigh reads 180°F/82°C. Baste the turkey frequently during cooking, adding a little more stock or water as necessary. Start checking on cooking progress after 3 hours by piercing the thigh with a skewer— the juices should run clear, if not, continue cooking. Cover the turkey with foil if it browns too quickly. Transfer it to a large plate and allow to stand, covered with a tent of foil, for at least 30 minutes.

9 Pour the cooking juices into a bowl and allow to stand 5 minutes, then skim off as much fat as possible, returning 3–4 tablespoons of fat to the roasting pan for making the giblet gravy. Set this over medium heat, add the flour and cook for about 2 minutes, stirring to blend the flour into the fat. Gradually whisk in the pan juices and the reserved giblet stock and bring to a boil, skimming off any foam that rises to the surface. Reduce the heat to medium-low and simmer the gravy for about 10 minutes, until slightly thickened and reduced. Season with salt and pepper and strain into gravy boats. Alternatively, if using the giblet meat, stir it into the gravy, heat through and then pour into gravy boats.

10 To serve, remove the skewers and spoon the stuffing into a serving bowl; keep warm. Carve the turkey on to a large heated platter or directly on to dinner plates and serve with stuffing, gravy, and all the trimmings.

Standing Rib Roast with Roast Potatoes

Serves 8-10

Rib-sticking fare? Cook him a special standing rib roast. It's a superb cut and makes an excellent special occasion meal. It is a good alternative to turkey for Christmas. Don't forget to make lots of potatoes—men can never seem to have enough of them.

4–6 beef rib roast (standing rib roast of
   beef), weighing about 6–8lb/2.75–3.6kg
olive or vegetable oil, for cooking
Dijon mustard, for brushing (optional)
5lb/2.5kg floury potatoes
1–2 tbsp/15–30g butter (optional)
2–3 tbsp all-purpose (plain) flour
1½–2 cups/375–500ml beef stock or water
salt and freshly ground black pepper
watercress, to garnish

1 Preheat the oven to 325°F (160°C/Gas 3). Rub the roast generously all over with olive or vegetable oil. Season well with salt and pepper and, if you like, brush with a little Dijon mustard. Transfer to a large, heavy-based roasting pan and add enough water to cover the base of the pan.

2 Insert a meat thermometer into the thickest part of the beef and roast for about 15 minutes per 1lb/450g for rare, 20 minutes per 1lb/450g for medium-rare, or longer for well done. The thermometer should read about 140°F/60°C for rare, 150°F/65°C for medium-rare, and 170°F/75°C for well done. Baste with the pan juices occasionally and add more water to the pan if the juices begin to burn.

3 About 1¼ hours before serving, cook the potatoes in simmering salted water for 5–7 minutes, until the outside of the potatoes are beginning to soften. Pour enough oil into another large roasting pan to cover the bottom generously and, if using, add the butter. Heat in the oven with the beef for about 5 minutes, until the butter has melted. Swirl the pan to mix the oil and butter, then place it over medium heat on top of the stove.

4 Drain the potatoes into a large colander and shake and toss them to 'rough up' their outsides. Carefully transfer to the roasting tray and turn each potato to coat with the oil mixture. Sprinkle with salt and roast in the oven for about 1 hour or until tender and golden, turning and basting frequently.

5 Transfer the beef to a platter and tent with foil, then allow to stand for 15–20 minutes. Increase the oven temperature to 375°F (190°C/Gas 5). Pour off as much fat as possible from the roasting pan and set the pan over medium-high heat. Add the flour and cook for 2–3 minutes, stirring constantly until smooth and well blended.

6 Gradually whisk in the stock or water and bring to a boil. Skim off any foam or impurities that rise to the surface and simmer the gravy for 8–10 minutes, stirring frequently, until thickened and smooth. Season with salt and pepper, if necessary, and strain into a gravy boat.

7 To serve, transfer the meat to a serving platter and garnish with the watercress. Transfer the potatoes to a warm serving bowl (drain on paper towels if necessary) and serve with the beef and gravy.

Châteaubriand with Béarnaise Sauce

Serves 2

Dazzle him with your sophistication, and bring the fine art of French cooking to your kitchen. During the 1950s, fish mousseline, cheese soufflé, beef Wellington, crêpes Suzette and this fabulous steak recipe became dinner party staples. Sauté potatoes and green beans go well with the steak.

1lb/450g beef tenderloin (fillet steak), about 6in/15cm long, cut from the thickest part
1 tbsp vegetable oil
watercress, to garnish

Béarnaise Sauce
2/3 cup/150g butter, cut into small pieces
2 tbsp dry white wine
2 tbsp tarragon vinegar or white wine vinegar
1 shallot, finely chopped
2 tbsp chopped tarragon or 1 tbsp dried tarragon
2 egg yolks
salt and freshly ground black pepper

1 Make the Béarnaise sauce first: gently melt the butter in a small saucepan over low heat without allowing it to boil. Skim off the foam from the surface and set aside.

2 Put the wine, vinegar, chopped shallot, and fresh or dried tarragon into a medium saucepan and bring to a boil over high heat. Boil until the liquid has almost evaporated leaving about 1 tablespoon in the pan. Remove from the heat and cool slightly.

3 Whisk the egg yolks into the reduced liquid in the pan for about 1 minute, until well blended and foamy. Replace pan over very low heat and whisk constantly. Begin to add the butter drop by drop, whisking until the yolk mixture begins to thicken. Gradually pour in the remaining butter in a slow, thin stream, leaving behind the milky white solids at the bottom of the pan. Season with salt and pepper and remove from the heat. Strain into a sauceboat, if required, or bowl and keep warm over hot water, stirring occasionally.

4 Preheat the broiler (grill). Place the meat between two sheets of plastic wrap (cling film) and pound with a meat mallet or rolling pin to flatten it slightly, until it is about 2in/5cm thick. Rub with the oil on all sides and season with salt and pepper.

5 Cook the beef on a foil-lined pan about 5 in/13cm from the heat and for 8–10 minutes, turning once, for rare; allow a few minutes longer for medium rare or longer to taste.

6 Transfer the beef to a board or dish and rest, covered, about 5 minutes. Carve the beef into slices, garnish with watercress and serve with the sauce.

COOK'S TIP
Though it traditionally accompanies steak, don't forget that béarnaise sauce is also delicious with fish. It is important to serve it as soon as possible after it has cooked, otherwise there is a risk that it might curdle or separate. Keep the sauce covered to prevent a skin from forming, and stir it frequently while you are cooking the steak.

Broiled T-Bone Steaks with Deep-Fried Onion Rings

Serves 4

You cannot get more 'regular guy' fare than steak and potatoes—especially when it's accompanied by deep-fried onion rings. This popular retro combination is still available in steak houses everywhere. Serve with baked, sautéed or French-fried potatoes.

2 large Spanish or other sweet onions, sliced
   into ¼in/5mm rings
4 steaks, such as T-bone or sirloin, each
   10–12oz/275–350g and 1in/2.5cm thick
Dijon mustard, for brushing (optional)
vegetable oil, for frying

Beer Batter

½ cup/55g all-purpose (plain) flour
2 tbsp cornstarch (cornflour)
salt and freshly ground black pepper
1 large egg, lightly beaten
½ cup / 125ml beer

1 To prepare the batter, sift the flour and cornstarch into a large bowl and stir in 1 teaspoon salt and a little pepper. Make a well in the ingredients and pour in the egg and beer. Using a fork, gently stir until the flour and liquids are just blended—do not over-mix as a few lumps of flour do not matter. Set aside.

2 Heat about 3in/7.5cm vegetable oil in a large saucepan or wok over medium-high heat to 180°F/350°C or until a cube of bread browns in about 30 seconds.

3 Preheat the broiler (grill) while cooking the onion rings. Working in batches, dip a few onion rings at a time into the batter, lift out and shake off any excess, then carefully drop them into the oil. Cook for about 45 seconds, until crisp and golden, turning once. Drain on paper towels and keep warm. Scoop out and discard any crusty bits of batter from the oil occasionally.

4 Arrange the steaks on a broiler tray and, if using, brush with a little Dijon mustard, then season with salt and pepper. Cook for 3–4 minutes on each side for rare, or longer for a medium or well-done steak. Transfer to four dinner plates and serve with the fried onion rings and your choice of potatoes.

Barbecued Teriyaki Steaks

½ cup/125ml bought teriyaki marinade

½ cup/125ml orange juice

2 garlic cloves, crushed

1 tsp grated fresh ginger root

4 green (spring) onions, finely chopped

1 tbsp dark brown sugar

hot pepper sauce, to taste

4 tenderloin (fillet) or sirloin steaks,
   each about 10oz/275g and at least
   1in/2.5cm thick

Serves 4

If your guy's an enthusiastic outdoor cook, he'll enjoy discovering a touch of the exotic for his barbecue repertoire. Teriyaki sauce is widely available in supermarkets; use it to give a wonderful flavor to many kinds of meat—including pork and chicken—as well as the steak used in this recipe.

1 In a deep dish large enough to hold the steaks, combine the teriyaki marinade, orange juice, garlic, ginger, green onions, brown sugar, and a few dashes of hot pepper sauce. Add the steaks to the marinade and turn to coat them completely. Cover and marinate at room temperature for about 2 hours or chill overnight. Turn the steaks occasionally.

2 Prepare an outdoor charcoal or gas barbecue or preheat the broiler (grill). Drain any excess marinade from the steaks and cook for 6–8 minutes (rare) or longer for medium or well-done, turning once and basting often with the marinade.

Beef Stew with Herb Dumplings

Serves 6

Serve him this heartwarming stew when he's been out and about on a cold winter's day. Adding tasty winter vegetables, like carrots, onions and butternut squash, contributes sweetness and richness. The dumplings are an essential feature and mashed potatoes go very well with the stew.

1/2 cup/55g all-purpose (plain) flour
salt and freshly ground pepper
3lb/1.5kg chuck steak or other stewing
  beef, cut into 2in/5cm cubes
about 4 tbsp vegetable oil
2 large onions, thinly sliced
1 cup/250ml fruity red wine
2 cups/500ml beef stock or water
1/2 cup/125ml tomato ketchup
2 garlic cloves, finely chopped

2 bay leaves
1 large bouquet garni
2–3 carrots, cut into 1/2in/1cm pieces
1lb/450g butternut or acorn squash,
  cut into chunks
10oz/275g pearl onions, peeled
1–2 tbsp chopped parsley, to garnish

Herb Dumplings

1 1/2 cups/175g all-purpose (plain) flour
1 1/2 tsp baking powder
1/2 tsp salt
3oz/75g beef or vegetable suet, grated
3–4 tbsp finely chopped mixed fresh
  herbs, such as parsley, thyme sage,
  dill, and chives
4–6 tbsp milk

1 Put the flour in a plastic bag and season with salt and pepper. Working in small batches, put a few cubes of beef in the bag, twist the bag closed and shake to coat the meat evenly. Transfer the meat to a plate and continue to coat the remainder.

2 Heat about 4 tablespoons oil over medium-high heat in a large heavy-based saucepan. Working in batches, brown the beef cubes evenly on all sides, about 7 minutes for each batch. Transfer to a plate and continue until all the beef is browned.

3 Add a little more oil, if necessary, then add the sliced onions. Cook for about 5 minutes, stirring, until softened. If you like a thicker stew, sprinkle over any remaining flour and cook for about 2 minutes, stirring to scrape up any browned bits from the bottom of the pan. Gradually whisk in the wine,

stock or water, ketchup, garlic, bay leaves and bouquet garni, and season to taste with salt and pepper.

4 Bring to a boil, skimming off any foam that rises to the surface. Replace the beef, reduce the heat to medium-low and simmer, covered, for $1^{1}/2-1^{3}/4$ hours, stirring occasionally, until the meat is almost tender. After simmering for 1 hour, stir in the carrots; and, after $1^{1}/4-1^{1}/2$ hours, stir in the butternut squash.

5 To prepare the dumplings, sift the flour, baking powder, and salt into a large bowl. Stir in the suet, mixed herbs, and salt with a little pepper. Add the milk, little by little, stirring to make a soft dough.

COOK'S TIP

To make a bouquet garni, tie together 2 small celery stalks, a few slices of leek, a large handful of parsley springs and several sprigs of fresh thyme.

6 Remove the bouquet garni from the stew and stir in the pearl onions. Using a large spoon, drop 8 large or 12 small balls of dumpling mixture into the stew. Simmer for about 20 minutes, covered, until the dumplings are puffed and slightly firm to the touch. Sprinkle with parsley and serve.

Old-Fashioned Meatloaf

Good old-fashioned home cooking is often referred to as 'meatloaf and mashed potatoes'—meaning tasty and comforting—and this delicious recipe is the perfect example. It may even be as good as his mom's! Meatloaf was often served with beets. Don't use lean ground beef or the loaf will be dry.

2 tbsp vegetable oil
1 large onion, finely chopped
1 carrot, grated
2 garlic cloves, chopped
2lb/900g ground (minced) beef
1½ cups/75g fresh white bread crumbs
2 eggs, lightly beaten
½ tsp dried thyme
2–4 tbsp finely chopped parsley
1 tbsp Worcestershire sauce
⅔ cup/150ml tomato ketchup,
  plus extra for glazing
salt and freshly ground
                  black pepper

1 Heat the oil in a frying pan. Add the onion and carrot and cook for about 5 minutes, stirring frequently, until the vegetables begin to soften. Stir in the garlic and cook for a further 1 minute. Remove from the heat and cool.

2 Preheat the oven to 350°F (180°C/Gas 4) and lightly oil a 9 x 5 x 3in/23 x 13 x 7.5cm loaf pan. In a large bowl, combine the beef, bread crumbs and cooled vegetable mixture. Add the eggs, thyme, parsley, Worcestershire sauce, ketchup and salt and pepper, then use a fork or your hands to mix the ingredients lightly together until just blended. Do not over work the mixture or the meatloaf will be too compact and dry.

3 Spoon the mixture into the pan, pressing gently to smooth the top. Bake for about 1¼ hours, until the edges begin to shrink from the sides of the pan. About 10 minutes before the meatloaf is done, brush the top with about 2 tablespoons ketchup to give it a glaze.

4 Set aside to cool for about 10 minutes, covered loosely with foil. Pour off any excess juices, if you like, before leaving the meatloaf to cool. To serve, turn out on to a dish or plate and cut into slices; alternatively, slice the meatloaf from the pan.

COOK'S TIP

For a rustic meatloaf, press the mixture into an oval leaf-shape and transfer to a shallow baking pan. Lay about 6 rindless bacon slices (rashers) across the loaf, tucking them under the edge. Bake as above, basting with the pan juices. Leave to stand for 10 minutes and pour off any excess juices before serving.

Baked Lasagne

Pasta is just the kind of food that satisfies a man's appetite. All kinds of Italian-style specialties became popular after World War II, many, such as pizza, spaghetti and meatballs, adapted to suit local tastes and ingredients. This delicious lasagne is made with a ricotta cheese mixture instead of white sauce, making it lighter and less rich. Garlic bread and a tossed salad are the standard accompaniments.

2 tbsp olive oil
1 onion, finely chopped
2 garlic cloves, crushed
1lb/450g ground (minced) beef
28oz/840g canned plum tomatoes
15oz/450g can tomato sauce or passata
2–3 tbsp tomato paste
1 tbsp finely chopped oregano
  or 1½ tsp dried oregano
1 tbsp finely chopped thyme
  or 1½ tsp dried thyme
1 tsp crushed red chilies
1 bay leaf
about 14 fresh or dried lasagne
  noodles (sheets)
2 eggs, lightly beaten
1lb/450g ricotta cheese
2 tbsp finely chopped parsley or basil
1lb/450g good-quality mozzarella cheese
salt and freshly ground black pepper
freshly grated Parmesan cheese,
  for sprinkling

1 Heat the oil over medium-high heat in a large saucepan or Dutch oven (flameproof casserole). Add the onion and cook, stirring frequently, until beginning to soften. Add the garlic and beef and cook, stirring to break up the beef, until browned.

2 Stir in the tomatoes, tomato sauce or passata, tomato paste, and salt and pepper. Add the oregano, thyme, chilies and bay leaf. Bring the sauce to a boil, stirring and pressing the tomatoes against the side of the pan to break them up. Reduce the heat to low and partially cover the pan, then simmer for about 45 minutes, stirring occasionally, until the sauce is thickened and slightly reduced. Remove the bay leaf.

3 If using fresh lasagne, no pre-cooking is necessary. For dried lasagne, bring a large, deep frying pan half-filled with salted water to a boil over high heat. Working in batches, cook the lasagne for 2–3 minutes, until just beginning to soften. Drain and lay out to dry on a clean dish towel.

4 Preheat the oven to 375°F (190°C/Gas 5). In a large bowl, beat the eggs and ricotta until blended. Season with salt and pepper and stir in the parsley or basil.

5 Spoon enough meat sauce into a deep baking dish about 9 x 13in/23 x 33cm just to cover the bottom. Cover the sauce with a layer of lasagne, overlapping or trimming the pieces to fit, if necessary. Spread about a third of the ricotta mixture on top and sprinkle with a little mozzarella, then cover with a layer of meat sauce. Continue the layers, ending with meat sauce and mozzarella. Sprinkle with freshly grated Parmesan cheese.

6 Transfer the dish to a baking sheet (to collect any drips) and bake for 45–55 minutes, until the lasagne is bubbling and crisp around the edges. Leave to stand for 5–10 minutes before serving.

Spaghetti and Meatballs

This has got to be one of his best-loved meals—the subject of songs as well as menus! It was taken around the world by the same Italian immigrants who introduced pizza and ice cream.

2 tbsp olive oil
1 onion, finely chopped
2 garlic cloves, crushed
2 tsp dried basil
1 tsp dried oregano
1/2 tsp dried thyme
1 cup/55g fresh white bread crumbs
1/4 cup/60ml whipping cream
1 egg, lightly beaten
1lb/450g ground (minced) beef
4oz/115g ground (minced) pork
4oz/115 ground (minced) veal
3/4 cup/55g grated Parmesan cheese
2 tbsp chopped parsley
salt and freshly ground black pepper

Tomato Sauce

2 tbsp olive oil
1 onion, finely chopped
2 garlic cloves, crushed
4 x 15oz/425g cans Italian
  tomato sauce
12oz/350g tomato paste
1 tbsp brown sugar
1 bay leaf
1 tsp dried oregano
1 tsp dried basil
2 tbsp chopped parsley

To Serve

1 tbsp vegetable oil
1lb/450g spaghetti

1 First make the tomato sauce: heat the oil in a heavy-based saucepan over medium heat. Add the onion and cook, stirring occasionally, until softened, about 8 minutes. Add the garlic and cook 1 minute.

2 Stir in the Italian tomato sauce, tomato paste, sugar, bay leaf, oregano, and basil. Bring to a boil, stirring occasionally, and season to taste with salt and pepper. Reduce the heat and simmer until slightly reduced and thickened, about 1 hour. Stir in the parsley.

3 Meanwhile, prepare the meatballs: heat the oil in a frying pan over medium heat. Add the onion and cook until softened, stirring occasionally. Add the garlic, basil, oregano, and thyme, and season to taste; cook 1 minute longer. Remove from the heat and allow to cool.

4 Put the bread crumbs in a bowl with the cream, and allow to stand until the cream is absorbed.

Beat in the egg. Mix the ground beef, pork, and veal in a large bowl using a fork or your fingertips. Add the onion mixture, the soaked bread, about a third of the Parmesan, and the parsley. Mix until well combined.

5 Shape the meat mixture into 1¹/₂ in/4cm meatballs. About 30 minutes before the tomato sauce is cooked, drop the meatballs into the simmering sauce and continue to cook, stirring occasionally.

6 Bring a large saucepan three-quarters full of water to a boil. Add 1 tablespoon salt and the oil. Add the spaghetti, stirring to separate the strands, and bring back to a boil. Cook for 8–10 minutes, until tender but still firm to the bite or *al dente*. Drain and transfer to warmed serving bowls. Top with a little sauce and some meatballs. Serve with the remaining grated Parmesan.

His Favorite Chili

Chili is one dish that is guaranteed to bring out the macho in the man and the man into the kitchen. Now an international dish and a Tex-Mex icon, all chili lovers have their 'perfect' recipe. There's a running debate about the spices, seasonings and beans that should be used—and even contests to judge the finest chilies (see below.)

2 tbsp vegetable oil
1 large onion, finely chopped
1 green bell pepper, seeded and chopped
2–4 garlic cloves, crushed
2 small jalapeño chilies, finely chopped
2lb/900g ground (minced) beef
2–4 tbsp mild or hot chili powder (or to taste)
4 x 14½oz/425g cans whole or chopped
 tomatoes
12oz/350g tomato paste
½ cup/125ml water
1 tbsp brown sugar

2 tsp salt ,or to taste
1 tsp dried thyme
1 tsp ground cumin
1 tsp ground cinnamon
cayenne pepper, to taste
15oz/425g can red kidney beans, drained
2 tbsp chopped fresh cilantro (coriander)
   or parsley

To Serve
boiled rice
sour cream, grated cheese, chopped
   jalapeño chilies, onions, and/or
   avocado (optional)

1 Heat the oil over medium heat in a heavy-based saucepan or Dutch oven (flameproof casserole). Add the onion, bell pepper, garlic, and chilies, and cook for about 8 minutes, until just softened, stirring frequently.

2 Add the ground beef to the pan, breaking it up with a spoon, and cook until no pink meat remains, about 10 minutes. Stir in the chili powder and cook 1 minute. Stir in the tomatoes, crushing them against the side of the pan if whole, tomato paste, water, sugar, salt, thyme, cumin, cinnamon, and cayenne pepper. Bring to a boil, stirring occasionally. Reduce the heat and simmer, partially covered, for about 1 hour, until slightly reduced. Stir occasionally during cooking.

3 Stir in the kidney beans and, if you like, season with extra cayenne pepper. Simmer, uncovered, for about 30 minutes, until thickened.

4 Stir in the chopped cilantro or parsley, and serve with rice and a selection of condiments.

Red Hot Barbecue Ribs

Serves 4–6

This is hot stuff—and he'll love it! In the 1960s Sylvia's of Harlem was the in place to eat barbecue ribs as well as collared greens, sweet potatoes and cornbread. Get the barbecue sauce right and the rest is easy—just bake or broil, or grill the ribs over hot coals for the most informal of fun meals.

2 tbsp vegetable oil
1 onion, finely chopped
4 garlic cloves, crushed
6 cloves
1 cinnamon stick
1/2 tsp ground cumin
1 cup/250ml tomato ketchup
1/2 cup/125ml sweet or hot chili sauce, or to taste
1/2 cup/125ml cider vinegar
1/2 cup/125ml soy sauce
1/3 packed cup/45g dark brown sugar
2 tbsp Worcestershire sauce
1 cup/250ml water
5lb/2.25kg pork spareribs, in sheets, preferably baby back ribs

To Serve
boiled corn-on-the-cob
cornbread
coleslaw or potato salad

1 Heat the oil in a saucepan over medium heat. Add the onion and cook for 4–5 minutes until soft, stirring occasionally. Add the garlic, cloves, cinnamon stick and cumin, and cook 1 minute longer. Stir in the tomato ketchup, chili sauce, cider vinegar, soy sauce, sugar, Worcestershire sauce, and water. Bring to a boil, reduce the heat and simmer until the sauce thickens to a coating consistency, stirring occasionally; add a little more water if necessary. Remove from the heat to cool slightly.

2 Preheat the oven to 300°F (150°C/Gas 2). Line a large roasting pan with foil and arrange the ribs in it in a single layer. Spoon the barbecue sauce evenly over the ribs and cover the pan with foil. Bake for about 45 minutes, basting occasionally with the sauce and juices.

3 Increase the oven temperature to 375°F (190°C/Gas 5). Remove the foil and return the ribs to the oven for 20–30 minutes longer, basting several times, until well glazed and browned. Alternatively, broil (grill) under medium-high heat or over hot coals on an outdoor barbecue, basting frequently, as above. Serve the ribs with any remaining barbecue sauce and corn-on-the-cob, cornbread, coleslaw, or potato salad.

Double-thick Fruity Stuffed Pork Chops

Serves 4

Mmm! He'll love these hunky pork chops. They were immensely popular in the 1960s and '70s as they were inexpensive and simple to cook, especially using bought seasonings, like 'Shake 'n' Bake', that made them even speedier and easier. These pork chops are aromatic with the same seasonings as traditional roast pork—sage, onion, and apple—and they are elegant enough for a special occasion. Ask the butcher to cut double-thick loin chops.

4 double-thick pork chops, preferably
 boneless loin chops, each weighing about
 12oz/350g, trimmed of fat.
2 tbsp vegetable oil
3/4 cup/185ml chicken stock
1/4 cup/60ml heavy (double) cream
2 tbsp finely chopped parsley
warm apple sauce, for serving

Stuffing

2 tbsp vegetable oil
1 small onion, finely chopped
1 small desert apple, peeled, cored and
 finely chopped
1 tsp dried sage
1–2 tsp Dijon mustard
3/4 cup/45g fresh white bread crumbs
3/4 cup/185ml apple cider or
 unsweetened juice
salt and freshly ground black pepper
2 tbsp coarsely chopped pecan nuts
 (optional)

1 To prepare the stuffing, heat the oil in a frying pan over medium heat. Add the onion and cook for 3 minutes. Add the apple and cook, stirring, for about 3 minutes longer, until just tender.

2 Remove from the heat and stir in the sage, mustard and bread crumbs. Drizzle in 2–3 tablespoons of the cider or juice or just enough to moisten the stuffing and bind it together. Season with salt and pepper and, if using, stir in the pecans. Set aside.

3 Using a small sharp knife, make a deep, horizontal slit in from the rounded outer edge of each chop to form a pocket, taking care not to slice right through the chop. Spoon an equal amount of stuffing into the pocket of each chop and secure with wooden toothpicks (cocktail sticks).

4 Heat the oil in a large, heavy-based frying pan over medium-high heat. Add the chops and cook until golden on both sides, about 4 minutes, turning once. Transfer to a plate.

5 Add the remaining cider or juice and bring to a boil, stirring to scrape up any cooking residue from the bottom of the pan. Return the pork chops to the pan and reduce the heat to low. Cover and simmer about 20 minutes, basting occasionally.

6 Transfer the chops to a warm serving dish and keep hot covered with foil. Increase the heat to high. Add the stock and bring to a boil, skimming off any foam. Reduce the liquid by about a third—this will take about 4 minutes.

7 Stir in the cream and any juices from the dish of chops. Reduce the heat to medium and simmer for 2–3 minutes, until the sauce is thickened slightly. Season with salt and pepper and either strain the sauce over the pork chops or serve it separately. Sprinkle with parsley and serve with apple sauce.

Baked Country Ham with Honey-Mustard Glaze

Country hams, such as Smithfield and Virginia are available in various national and regional styles. They are traditionally served at Easter, sometimes for New Year and for party buffets. They require soaking, scrubbing, and boiling before baking, then most recipes use a sweet glaze to complement the rich ham.

10–12lb/4.9–6kg fully cooked whole ham, preferably boneless
whole cloves, for studding

Honey-Mustard Glaze

2 tbsp soy sauce
1/4 cup/60ml water
1 cup/250ml clear honey
1/2 cup/125ml Dijon mustard
1/2–1 tsp cornstarch (cornflour)

1 Preheat the oven to 325°F (160°C/Gas 3). Place the ham on a rack in a large roasting pan and add enough water to cover the bottom of the pan. Insert a meat thermometer in the thickest part of the ham and roast, uncovered, allowing 20–25 minutes per 1lb/450g or until the thermometer reaches 160°F/70°C. Add more water if needed during cooking as the moisture from this prevents the ham from drying out.

2 About 1 hour before the ham is due to be ready, combine the soy sauce, water, honey, and mustard for the glaze in a small saucepan. Bring to the boil over medium heat, stirring, and then remove from the heat.

3 Remove the ham from the oven and, with a sharp knife, carefully remove the rind, leaving about 1/2 in/5 mm layer of white fat. Slash the surface of the fat diagonally to create a diamond pattern and press a clove in the middle of each diamond. Carefully brush with the glaze and continue to roast for a further 45 minutes, brushing with more glaze occasionally. Keep the bottom of the roasting pan covered with water to prevent the sweet glaze drippings from scorching. Transfer the ham to a serving platter and tent it with foil but do not let the foil stick to the glazed surface. Set aside.

4 Tilt the roasting pan and skim off any fat from the pan drippings, then add the remaining glaze to the pan and set it over medium heat. Stir 2–3 tablespoons water into the cornstarch until smooth, then stir it into the glaze and bring to a boil, stirring, until lightly thickened. Add more blended cornstarch or water, as necessary, and add any juices from the baked ham. Strain into a gravy boat.

5 Garnish the ham with parsley and serve hot, with boiled or mashed potatoes, and the glaze as a sauce. Alternatively, serve at room temperature with a selection of salads.

hunky crunchy 'n fresh

These great dishes are just right for keeping
your man healthy and hunky—and he'll also
be happy because they all taste so good.
Crunchy Waldorf Salad, and Spinach and
Mushroom Salad with Hot Bacon Dressing are
full of raw goodness in punchy dressings—just
eating them works up a healthy glow. Some
dishes are full of comforting simplicity, and on
that score it is hard to beat Twice-Baked
Potatoes or Maple-baked Acorn Squash. Sweet
Potato Casserole with Marshmallow Topping is
the stuff that childhood memories are made of—
gooey and gorgeous!

Whole Artichokes with Melted Butter and Lemon

Whet his appetite and butter him up at the same time with this simple but delicious vegetable starter. Artichokes began to achieve their international popularity in the '60s. This Mediterranean native is now familiar in many countries—not only in France or Italy. In fact Castroville, California, calls itself the artichoke capital of the world!

Serves 2

2 globe artichokes,
  about 10oz/275g
  each
1 lemon, halved
¼ cup/60g butter
1 tbsp lemon juice,
  or to taste
2 tbsp chopped
  parsley

1 Holding the side of the globe artichoke against a work surface with the stem overhanging the edge, press down firmly on the stem to break it off. Breaking, rather than cutting, helps to pull out any tough strings of vegetable. Using a sharp knife, cut the bottom evenly to create a flat base.

2 Carefully cut off about 1in/2.5cm straight across the top of each artichoke. Pull off any loose or brown leaves from around the bottom, then use kitchen scissors to trim off the sharp leaf tips.

3 Bring a large saucepan half-filled with water to the boil over high heat and add the artichokes. Squeeze the juice from the lemon and reserve 1 tablespoon for the sauce, then add the rest to the artichokes. Add the lemon halves to the pan. Reduce the heat to medium-low and simmer for 20–25 minutes or until a leaf pulls out easily. Remove the artichokes and drain upside down on a rack.

4 In a small saucepan, melt the butter and reserved lemon juice over low heat. Stir in the parsley and divide between two small bowls or ramekins. Arrange the artichokes cut-side up and serve with the butter sauce.

EATING COOKED ARTICHOKES

Pull off the leaves one at a time and dip them into the sauce. Draw the bottom end of the leaf through your teeth to remove the tender flesh. Discard the remainder of the leaf. Continue eating the leaves until the clump of pale leaves covering the fuzzy 'choke' is exposed. Discard the clump of leaves and use a teaspoon to scoop out and discard the choke, then eat the remaining bottom with a knife and fork, dipping each piece into the sauce.

Eggplant Parmigiana

Serves 6

He'll love this classic Italian dish. Enterprising restaurants, with their influx of cosmopolitan customers, introduced unfamiliar vegetables such as eggplants to American cooking. Delmonico's was one restaurant that became famous for its European-style cooking using sophisticated ingredients.

olive oil, for frying
2 eggs, beaten with 1 tbsp water
1 cup/65g natural dried bread crumbs
1 large or 2 medium eggplants (aubergines),
  cut across into ½in/1cm slices
½ cup/45g freshly grated Parmesan cheese
2 cups/225g mozzarella cheese, preferably
  buffalo, thinly sliced

Tomato Sauce
2 tbsp olive oil
1 large onion, finely chopped
2–3 garlic cloves, minced
2 x 14½–16oz/425g cans chopped tomatoes
2 tsp brown sugar
1 bay leaf
1 tsp dried oregano
1 tsp dried basil
2 tbsp shredded fresh basil
salt and freshly ground black pepper
mixed-leaf salad, to serve

1 First prepare the tomato sauce: heat the oil in a heavy-based saucepan over medium heat. Add the onion and cook for about 7 minutes, until the onion is soft and translucent, stirring occasionally.

2 Add the garlic and cook for a further 1 minute, then add the tomatoes, sugar, bay, oregano and dried basil, and bring to a boil, stirring frequently. Reduce the heat and simmer, stirring occasionally, until the sauce has thickened, about 30–45 minutes. Season with salt and pepper, stir in the fresh basil, and remove from the heat. Set aside.

3 Grease a large, shallow baking dish with a little olive oil and set this aside. Put the beaten egg in a shallow dish and the bread crumbs on a sheet of waxed (greaseproof) paper. Dip slices of eggplant into the egg mixture and then into the bread crumbs to coat each side completely.

4 In a heavy-based frying pan, heat 2–3 tablespoons olive oil over medium heat. Cook a few eggplant slices at a time, turning and cooking evenly, until golden, adding more oil if needed. Drain on paper towels. Repeat with all the slices.

5 Preheat the oven to 350°F (180°C/Gas 4). Spoon a little tomato sauce into the bottom of the dish and spread it evenly. Arrange a layer of eggplant slices over the sauce, sprinkle with a little Parmesan, and top with a layer of mozzarella slices, then cover with another layer of sauce.

6 Repeat the layers, ending with a thin layer of tomato sauce and a sprinkle of Parmesan. Drizzle a little olive oil on top and bake until bubbling and brown, about 35 minutes. Serve with a fresh mixed-leaf salad.

Sweet Potato Casserole with Marshmallow Topping

A favorite side dish of the 1950s and '60s, this combination of cooked sweet potatoes, brown sugar and mallows has been popular since before the American War of Independence! No Thanksgiving could be celebrated without this melt-in-the mouth casserole to accompany the turkey; it also goes well with Baked Country Ham with Honey-Mustard Glaze (see page 87).

Serves 6

8 medium sweet potatoes
1/3 packed cup/45g dark brown sugar
1/4 cup/30g butter
freshly grated nutmeg
3/4 tsp ground cinnamon
3/4 tsp ground allspice
freshly squeezed juice of 1/2 orange
salt and freshly ground black pepper
marshmallows, for topping

1 Peel the sweet potatoes and put them in a large saucepan or Dutch oven (flameproof casserole). Cover with cold water and bring to a boil over high heat. Reduce the heat to medium and simmer for about 30 minutes, until the potatoes are tender. Drain and transfer to a large bowl.

2 Meanwhile, preheat the oven to 375°F (190°C/Gas 5). Using a potato masher, mash the potatoes until smooth. Alternatively, put the potatoes through a potato ricer or food mill, or beat with an electric mixer. Add the sugar, butter, nutmeg to taste, cinnamon, allspice, orange juice , and salt and pepper, and beat until smooth and well blended.

3 Spoon the mixture into a 1 1/2 quart/1.5lt baking dish and arrange the marshmallows in rows across the surface, pressing them gently into the potato mixture. Bake for 10–15 minutes, until the potatoes are hot and bubbling and the marshmallows are golden and soft.

Maple-Baked Acorn Squash

Serves 4

Winter squashes, such as acorn, butternut and pumpkin, are available just at the right time for the New England maple syrup harvest. The syrup sweetly complements these popular winter vegetables. This recipe is one he'll just love—not only do the maple syrup and spices taste superb with the squash but acorn squash halves also look beautiful.

2 medium or small acorn squash
2 tbsp/30g butter
¼ cup/60ml pure natural maple syrup
  or light brown sugar
¼ tsp salt
¼ tsp ground cinnamon
⅛ tsp allspice
¼ cup/25g chopped pecan nuts or
  walnuts (optional)

1 Preheat the oven to 350°F (180°C/Gas 4).

2 Cut each squash across in half, then scoop out their seeds and fibers. Use a sharp knife to slice off a small piece of each base. Arrange the squash halves cut side down in a baking dish and cover with foil. Bake for about 30 minutes, until the squash begins to soften.

3 Turn the squash cut sides up and divide the butter, maple syrup and spices equally among them. If using, sprinkle each with nuts. Bake, uncovered, for about 20 minutes or until the squash are tender.

COOK'S TIP

Try using small butternut squashes and cutting them in half lengthwise.

95

Twice-Baked Potatoes

If your man is a keen gardener, he may bring you his own home-grown potatoes. Say "Thank you!" with this wonderful recipe. Baked potatoes with crispy skin have been popular for generations and were often cooked on top of the gas stove on a special potato baker. It was a kind of covered flat frying pan with a perforated plate to soften the flame. The smell of the crisping skins was wonderful and they tasted much better than potatoes baked in the oven. Originally they were topped with sliced cheese, but you could try grated Cheddar or Parmesan, chives or crumbled bacon, or even mozzarella and olive oil.

Serves 6

6 medium baking potatoes, well scrubbed
3 tbsp/45g butter
1/3 cup/75ml whipping cream or milk
salt and freshly ground white or
  black pepper

Topping
choose from grated Cheddar,
  Parmesan,
  or sliced American cheese;
  snipped chives; crumbled crisp-
  cooked bacon; crumbled blue
  cheese or diced mozzarella with
  olive oil instead of butter
paprika or cayenne (optional)

1 Preheat the oven to 375°F (190°C/Gas 5). Place the potatoes directly on the middle oven rack and bake for about 1 hour or until tender. Transfer to a cutting board. Increase the oven temperature to 450°F (230°C/Gas 8).

2 Using a kitchen cloth to protect your hand, cut a slice from along the top of each potato. Scoop the potato flesh from the slice and place it in a bowl; discard the top skin. Scoop out the flesh from the potatoes and add to the bowl.

3 Mash the potato with the butter, salt and pepper, and cream or milk until smooth. Spoon the mixture back into the potato shells and sprinkle each with the chosen topping. Place the filled potatoes on a baking sheet or dish and bake for 20–30 minutes, until golden. If you like, sprinkle with a little paprika or cayenne before serving.

Hunky, Crunchy 'n Fresh **97**

Chef's Salad

This popular salad originated as a recipe for using up leftovers. It is now a staple of every diner and lunch stop in any American town or city.

Serves 4

2 heads soft or butterhead lettuce, trimmed
8oz/225g honey-baked ham, cut into strips
8oz/225g cooked chicken or turkey breast, cut into strips
8oz/225g Emmental or Monterey Jack cheese, cut into strips
8 cherry tomatoes, quartered
4 hard-cooked eggs, quartered

Dressing

2 tbsp lemon juice or white wine vinegar
1 tbsp Dijon mustard
1 garlic clove, crushed
1 tsp sugar (optional)
1/4 cup/60ml vegetable oil
2–3 tbsp extra-virgin olive oil
salt and freshly ground black pepper

1 First make the dressing: put the lemon juice or white wine vinegar in a small bowl with the mustard, salt and pepper, garlic, and sugar, if using. Stir to blend well. Slowly pour in the vegetable oil in a thin stream, whisking constantly until a smooth, creamy dressing begins to form. Continue whisking while adding the olive oil in the same way until the dressing is thickened and smooth. Set aside.

2 Leave any small lettuce leaves whole and tear large leaves into smaller pieces, then divide evenly among four individual salad bowls or place on a large shallow platter.

3 Arrange the ham, chicken or turkey, and cheese strips on top of the lettuce, radiating from the middle to resemble wheel spokes and keeping even spaces between each ingredient. Fill the spaces with the tomato and egg quarters. Drizzle the salad dressing over and serve.

Caesar Salad

Inform your guy that this famous retro salad was popular with all the handsome Hollywood movie stars who visited Caesar's Palace in Tijuana, the Mexican border town. Created by Caesar Cardini in 1924, it is currently experiencing a revival. The famous dressing, which did not originally contain anchovies, is still sold as 'Cardini's Original' dressing mix.

1 egg, at room temperature
4–7 tbsp olive oil
1 tbsp/ 15g butter
1 garlic clove, crushed
3–4oz/ 75–115g French bread,
  cut into small cubes
2 tbsp lemon juice
freshly ground black pepper
1 large or 2 small heads Romaine (Cos)
  lettuce, torn into bite-size pieces
4 tbsp freshly grated Parmesan cheese,
  plus long curls or shreds to garnish
3 good-quality anchovy fillets,
  cut up (optional)

1 To coddle the egg, bring a small saucepan of water to a boil over high heat. Carefully slide the egg into the water and remove the pan from the heat. Cover and allow to stand for 1 minute.

2 In a medium frying pan, heat 1–2 tablespoons olive oil and the butter over medium-high heat. Add the garlic and the bread cubes and cook for 2–3 minutes, tossing and stirring, until the bread is golden on all sides. Remove from the heat and set the croûtons aside.

3 Put the lemon juice in a large salad bowl and add 3–5 tablespoons olive oil. Crack the egg into the bowl and whisk it into the lemon juice and oil until blended and creamy. Season with pepper, then add the lettuce and grated Parmesan and toss to coat. Add the anchovies, if using. Sprinkle over the croûtons. Garnish with Parmesan curls or shreds and serve.

NOTE
Raw and/or undercooked eggs should not be eaten by the elderly, the young or immuno-suppressed individuals.

Spinach and Mushroom Salad with Hot Bacon Dressing

Serves 4

In an era when salads were mainly for ladies who lunched, this was one of the first robust leafy dishes to pass the man-appeal test. Punchy bacon, garlic, and mustard are irresistible with little leaves and tender mushrooms.

1lb/450g baby spinach leaves,
  washed and dried
4oz/120g white mushrooms, thinly sliced
2 tbsp vegetable oil or bacon drippings
4 rindless bacon slices (rashers), cut into
  thin shreds

4 green (spring) onions, thinly sliced,
  or 2 tbsp snipped chives
1 garlic clove, crushed
1 cup/250ml cider vinegar or wine vinegar
1/2 tsp salt
1/2 tsp dry mustard powder
freshly ground black pepper

1 Toss the spinach leaves and sliced mushrooms in a large, heatproof salad bowl. In a heavy based frying-pan, heat the oil or drippings over medium heat. Add the bacon and cook until crisp and brown, stirring frequently. Drain on a paper towel.

2 Add the green onions and garlic to the pan, and cook over low heat until softened, stirring frequently. Stir in the vinegar, salt, and dry mustard, and season with black pepper. Bring to a boil, and carefully pour over the leaves. Sprinkle the bacon on top and toss lightly to mix. Serve immediately.

Waldorf Salad

This all-time classic is named after New York's Waldorf Astoria Hotel where the salad was created in the 1890s. Celery and apple were the original ingredients tossed in mayonnaise—the walnuts and dried fruit were added by successive generations of cooks.

Serves 4

4 celery stalks, thinly sliced
2 large red apples, quartered,
  cored and diced
1 cup/120g walnuts, chopped
1/2 cup/120g chopped soft dates or figs
  (optional)

about 1 cup/225g mayonnaise
lettuce leaves, for serving
pecan nut halves or apple slices, to garnish

1 Combine the celery, apples, and walnuts in a bowl, and, if using, the dates or figs. Gradually stir in enough mayonnaise to hold the ingredients together.

2 Arrange the lettuce leaves on a plate and heap the salad on them. Garnish with pecan halves or apple slices.

sweets
for your
sweetie

There's nothing like a serving of hot, sweet, and spicy apple pie to bring out the boy in the man. The amazing part is that it is always the good little boy that shines through—the one who knew that being lovable and appreciative was the best way of getting seconds. These retro desserts will bring whoops of joy when they are served up. What's more, they are just so much fun to cook—and fill the house with glorious aromas. Remember Hot Fudge Sundaes, Deluxe Banana Splits, creamy Chocolate Pudding, zesty Key Lime Pie, and New England Blueberry Pancakes? Make someone feel special by turning out the perfect sweet and share the feel-good sensation too.

Double-Crust Apple Pie

Make him an apple pie and show him that you love him—it'll remind him of his mom and all the memories of childhood evoked by the sweet, spicy aromas of home baking. Apple pie is immensely popular—most diners and roadside restaurants have one on the menu. Nothing beats a good homemade version, however.

Serves 6–8

2lb/900g cooking apples, peeled, cored, and sliced
1 tbsp lemon juice
1 cup/225g sugar, plus extra for sprinkling
2 tbsp all-purpose (plain) flour
1/2–1 tsp ground cinnamon
freshly grated nutmeg
1 tbsp/15g butter, for dotting
vanilla ice cream, to serve (optional)

Pie Crust

2 cups/225g all-purpose (plain) flour, sifted
1 tsp sugar
1/2 tsp salt
1/2 cup/120g unsalted butter, cut into pieces
3 tbsp/45g white vegetable shortening (white vegetable fat), chilled
1 tbsp lemon juice
1 egg yolk
4–6 tbsp ice water
1 egg, lightly beaten, to glaze

1 To make the pie crust, put the flour, sugar, and salt into a food processor and pulse once or twice to blend. Sprinkle in the butter pieces and shortening and process for about 10 seconds until the mixture resembles coarse crumbs.

4 Preheat the oven to 425°F (220°C/Gas 7). Lightly grease a 9in/23cm pie plate. Put the apples in a large bowl as they are prepared and sprinkle with the lemon juice; toss gently to combine. In a small bowl, mix the sugar, flour, cinnamon and some freshly grated nutmeg until combined. Sprinkle over the apples and toss to coat the fruit; set aside.

5 Unwrap one dough round and place on a lightly floured surface. Roll out the dough from the middle towards the edge, turning it by a quarter turn as you roll to keep it in a round shape. The dough should be about 1/8in/3mm thick. Gently ease the dough into the pie plate, pressing it in gently. Trim the excess, leaving 1/2in/1cm overlapping the edge. Brush the edge of the pastry with water and spoon the filling into the pie, mounding it slightly, then dot evenly with the butter.

6 Roll out the second dough round as before and place over the filling. With a sharp knife, cut a few slashes into the top to allow steam to escape. Trim the edge of the dough cover to the rim of the pie plate and turn the overhanging dough underneath up over the edge. Press to seal and crimp the edge. Brush with beaten egg. If you like, re-roll the trimmings and cut decorative leaves and fruits. Arrange on the pie and glaze again. Sprinkle with a little sugar.

7 Bake for about 25 minutes. Cover the edges of the pie with strips of foil to prevent them from over-browning and continue to bake for 20–25 minutes longer until the crust is set and golden and the filling is tender and bubbling.

8 Allow the pie to cool for at least 30 minutes before serving. The pie is delicious with vanilla ice cream.

2 With the machine running, add the egg yolk, lemon juice, and the water little by little, until the dough begins to come together. Do not allow the dough to form a ball around the blade or it will be tough. Press a little of the dough between your thumb and forefinger: if it does not hold together, add a little more water.

3 Remove the dough and divide it in half. Flatten the pieces into circles and wrap each in plastic wrap (cling film), then chill for 1–2 hours. Allow to soften slightly at room temperature before rolling.

Pumpkin Pie

This pie has been a favorite since colonial days—the abundance of pumpkins in the New World was its original source of inspiration. The pie regained popularity during the 1950s once canned pumpkin was easily available.

1½ cups/175g all-purpose (plain) flour
1 tsp sugar
½ tsp salt
½ cup/120g unsalted butter, cut into pieces
2 tbsp/25g white vegetable shortening
  (white vegetable fat), chilled
4–6 tbsp ice water
whipped cream, to serve

Filling
16oz/500g can pumpkin
¾ cup/175g sugar
1 tsp ground cinnamon
½ tsp ground ginger
½ tsp freshly grated nutmeg
½ tsp salt
3 eggs, lightly beaten
5⅓ oz/155g can evaporated milk
½ cup/125ml milk

1 Put the flour, sugar and salt into a food processor and pulse once or twice to blend. Sprinkle in the butter pieces and process for about 10 seconds, until the mixture resembles coarse crumbs. With the machine running, add the water, little by little, until the dough begins to come together but do not allow it to form a ball around

the blade or it will be tough. Press a little of the dough between your thumb and forefinger—if it does not hold together, add a little more water. Wrap in plastic wrap (cling film) and knead gently four or five times, then flatten the dough, wrap it securely, and chill for 1–2 hours. Allow to soften slightly at room temperature before rolling.

2 Lightly grease a 9in/23cm pie plate. Roll out the dough on a lightly floured surface to about 1/8in/3mm thick, working from the middle towards the edge. Turn the dough by a quarter turn occasionally as you roll to keep it in a round shape.

3 Gently ease the dough into the pie plate. Trim off the excess, leaving 1/2in/1cm overhanging the rim. Fold the overhanging dough under and pinch the edge up, then crimp it between your fingers. Alternatively, trim off all excess and re-roll the trimmings, then cut out leaves or other shapes. Brush the edge with water and press the cut-outs on to the edge. Prick the bottom of the pastry with a fork and chill for 30 minutes.

4 Preheat the oven to 375°F (190°C/Gas 5). Drain the pumpkin and place in a large bowl, then stir to break up the pieces. Using an electric beater, beat in the sugar, cinnamon, ginger, nutmeg, salt, and eggs. Add the evaporated milk and milk, and beat until smooth.

5 Pour the mixture into the pie, place on a baking sheet and bake for about 25 minutes. Cover the edges of the pastry with strips of foil and bake for about 30 minutes longer or until a knife inserted near the middle comes out clean. Leave to cool. Serve warm or chilled with whipped cream.

Georgia Pecan Pie

Remind him of a great tradition with one of the oldest and best-known retro desserts. Pecan pie evolved from 'transparent pie' made with molasses when the nuts were added to the sweet and sticky mixture. With melt-in-the-mouth cream cheese pastry, this is to die for!

1 1/2 cups/175g all-purpose (plain) flour
3oz/75g cream cheese, softened
1/2 cup/120g butter, softened
2 tbsp sugar

Filling

3–3 1/2 cups/250–275g pecan halves
3 eggs, lightly beaten
1 packed cup/225g dark brown sugar
1/2 cup/175g corn (golden) syrup
grated peel and juice of 1/2 lemon
4 tbsp/60g butter, melted and cooled
2 tsp vanilla extract
whipped cream or vanilla ice cream,
  to serve (optional)

1 Sift the flour into a large bowl. Add the cream cheese, butter, and sugar and, using a pastry blender or your fingertips, rub the cheese and butter into the flour until fine crumbs form. Pour into a 9in/23cm pie plate and pat on to the bottom and up the side, making the top edge even with the lip of the pan. (Alternatively, form the dough into a ball; flatten, wrap, and chill for about 1 hour. Roll out on a lightly floured surface and carefully line the pie plate.) Crimp the edge and chill.

2 Preheat the oven to 350°F (180°C/Gas 4). For the filling, pick out about a third of the pecans, selecting perfect halves and set aside. Coarsely chop the remaining pecans.

3 Whisk the eggs and brown sugar until light and foamy. Beat in the corn syrup, lemon peel and juice, melted butter, and vanilla extract. Stir in the chopped pecans and pour into the pie plate. Set the pie plate on a baking sheet, and carefully arrange the reserved pecan halves in concentric circles on the filling.

4 Bake until the filling is puffed and set and the pecans are browned, about 45 minutes. Leave to cool to room temperature. Serve with whipped cream or vanilla ice cream, if liked.

White Chocolate Amaretto Cheesecake

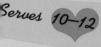

Serves 10–12 A New York restaurant, Lindy's, popularized this type of cheesecake in the 1940s. Baked in the sweet crust, the creamy filling can be tangy with lemon or rich and irresistible with chocolate, as here. Men love this cheesecake!

16–18 Graham crackers (digestive biscuits)
3–4 Amaretti cookies
¼ cup/50g butter, melted
½ tsp almond extract
½ tsp ground cinnamon

Filling

12oz/350g good-quality white
  chocolate, melted
½ cup/125ml heavy (double) cream
1½lb/675g cream cheese, softened
⅓ cup/65g sugar
4 eggs
1 tbsp Amaretto or ½ tsp almond extract
½ tsp vanilla extract

Topping

1¾ cups/440ml sour cream
¼ cup/50g sugar
1 tbsp Amaretto or ½ tsp almond extract
white chocolate curls, to decorate

1 Preheat the oven to 350°F (180°C/Gas 4). Grease a 9 x 3in/23 x 7.5cm springform pan. In a food processor, pulse the crackers (digestive biscuits) and Amaretti cookies into fine crumbs. Add the butter, almond extract, and cinnamon and blend. Press the crumbs on to the bottom and sides of the pan. Bake for 5–7 minutes to set the crust. Reduce the heat to 300°F (150°C/Gas 2).

2 For the filling, melt the chocolate and cream in a saucepan over low heat, stirring until smooth. Set aside until cool, stirring occasionally.

3 Using an electric mixer, beat the cream cheese until smooth. Gradually add the sugar, then each egg, beating well after each addition. Slowly beat in the melted chocolate mixture, the Amaretto or almond extract, and the vanilla extract.

4 Turn the filling into the biscuit crust, place on a baking sheet, and bake for 45–55 minutes until the edge of the cake is firm, but the middle is slightly soft. Increase the oven temperature to 400°F (200°C/Gas 6).

5 For the topping, whisk the sour cream, sugar, and the Amaretto or almond extract. Spread over the cheesecake. Return to the oven and bake for 5–7 minutes. Turn off the oven, but leave the cheesecake in it for 1 hour. Remove from the oven and leave to cool. Run a sharp knife between the crust and the side of the cake pan to loosen the cheesecake. Cover loosely and chill overnight.

6 To serve, unclip and remove the pan ring. Transfer to a serving plate and decorate with white chocolate curls.

Orange Chiffon Pie

In the 1950s, ready-prepared frozen pie shells began appearing in supermarkets, and their chiffon fillings—gelatin mixtures lightened with meringue—were quickly made from instant 'Jell-O' packaged desserts. These were whipped up to fill the pie shells and became incredibly popular—a true convenience dessert. Making a chiffon pie from scratch is almost as quick and easy, as it needs no cooking at all.

Serves 6–8

Crumb Crust
18–20 Graham crackers (digestive biscuits), finely crushed
4 tbsp/55g butter, melted
2 tbsp superfine (caster) sugar (optional)

Orange Chiffon Filling
¼ cup/60ml cold water
1 package or 1 tbsp gelatin
4 eggs, separated
1¼ cups/275g superfine (caster) sugar
grated peel of 1 orange
½ cup/125ml freshly squeezed orange juice
¼ tsp cream of tartar

To Decorate
julienne strips of orange peel, simmered in water until tender
whipped cream

1 To make the crumb crust, combine the crushed crackers, melted butter and sugar, if using, in a large bowl. Pour into a 9in/23cm pie pan and, using an 8in/20cm pie pan, press the crumbs firmly against the bottom and side of the larger pan. Alternatively, use the back of a tablespoon to press the crumbs evenly against the bottom and side of the pan. Chill until firm.

2 For the filling, pour the water into a coffee cup or small bowl, sprinkle over the gelatin and allow to stand for 10 minutes. Set the cup in a saucepan of just simmering water and heat gently for 5 minutes, stirring until the gelatin has completely dissolved.

COOK'S TIP

Instead of heating the softened gelatin in a pan of hot water, heat it in a microwave on high for 10–15 seconds and then stir until completely dissolved.

3 Using an electric beater, beat the egg yolks in a large heatproof bowl for 1–2 minutes, until light and fluffy. Gradually beat in half the sugar, the grated orange peel, and juice. Set the bowl over a saucepan of just simmering water (the bottom of the bowl should just touch the water) and cook, stirring constantly, for about 8–10 minutes, until the mixture thickens and coats the back of a wooden spoon. Remove the bowl from the water, stir in the gelatin mixture and cool this custard, stirring occasionally. If you like, set the custard over a bowl of cold water to cool quickly, but do not allow it to set.

4 Using clean beaters, whisk the egg whites and cream of tartar in a large bowl until fluffy. Increase the speed and whisk until soft peaks form. Gradually whisk in the remaining sugar until the whites are stiff and glossy.

5 Beat a spoonful of the whites into the cooled custard, then pour the custard mixture over the whites and fold together until the mixtures are just blended. Do not overwork the mixture—it does not matter if a few lumps of white remain. Pour into the crumb crust, mounding the mixture in the middle, and chill for 4–6 hours or until set.

6 Decorate with julienne strips of orange peel and serve with whipped cream.

Key Lime Pie

Remind him of happy, sunny vacations with this great, fresh-tasting dessert.
Florida Keys gave the world this deliciously tangy, lime-flavored pie that was as much the busy housewife's dream for its simplicity as her husband's for its divine flavor.

Serves 6-8

1½ cups/75g crushed vanilla wafers or langue de chat biscuits (about 35)
2–3 tbsp superfine (caster) sugar
⅓ cup/75g butter, melted

Filling

8oz/225g can sweetened condensed milk
½ cup/125ml freshly squeezed lime juice
3 egg yolks

To Decorate

1 cup/250ml heavy (double) cream, whipped
grated lime peel (optional)

1 Lightly grease a 9in/23cm pie plate. Mix the biscuit crumbs with the sugar and butter.

2 Pour the crumbs into the pie plate and, using the back of a spoon, press them evenly over the bottom and side. Chill until set.

3 To make the filling, whisk the condensed milk, lime juice, and egg yolks until well blended and thickened. Pour into the crust and chill until set. Decorate with a little whipped cream and, if desired, lime peel. Serve with additional whipped cream.

Chocolate Pudding

Serves 4—6

Chocolate pudding was so popular in the 1950s, '60s, and '70s that package mixes became available to make it at home. The pudding was literally child's play to make, and everyone used the mixes. Men adore chocolate pudding, and it is just as easy to make him an original from scratch.

2/3 cup/175g sugar
1/4 cup/30g cornstarch (cornflour)
1/4 tsp salt
1/4 tsp ground cinnamon (optional)
1 1/2 cups/375ml milk
1/2 cup/125ml whipping cream
4 tbsp/55g butter, cut into pieces
3 1/2oz/90g unsweetened (dark plain) chocolate, chopped
1 egg
1 tsp vanilla extract

To Decorate
whipped cream
chocolate shavings

1 Stir together the sugar, cornstarch, salt, and cinnamon, if using, in a large heavy-based saucepan and gradually whisk in the milk. Add the cut up butter and chopped chocolate and set over medium heat. Cook until the chocolate melts and the mixture thickens, whisking frequently. Bring to a boil and boil for 1 minute. Remove from the heat.

2 Beat the egg in a small bowl. Stir in a spoonful of the hot chocolate mixture, whisking constantly. Slowly pour the egg into the chocolate mixture, whisking constantly to prevent lumps from forming—the mixture will be very thick. Remove from the heat.

3 Strain the mixture into a large measuring cup or pitcher, pressing to push the thick mixture through, and stir in the vanilla extract.

4 Pour or spoon the pudding into dessert dishes, custard cups, or ramekins and cool. Cover and chill for 2 hours or overnight. Serve decorated with whipped cream and a few chocolate shavings on top.

Stove-Top Rice Pudding with Dried Fruit

Reassure him that life is still good with this rich, creamy rice pudding. It is one of the best home-cooked desserts that can be found in most diners and family restaurants. Use pudding rice or risotto rice for a pudding with a thick comforting texture.

Serves 4-6

4 cups/1lt milk
3/4 cup/140g dried cherries, dried
  cranberries, raisins, or golden raisins
  (sultanas), or a mixture
3–4 strips orange peel
1 cinnamon stick
1 cup/225g short-grain rice, such as
  pudding rice or risotto rice
1 cup/250ml heavy (double) cream
1/2 cup/120g sugar
1 tsp vanilla extract
1/4 tsp salt

To Serve
cinnamon sugar, brown sugar,
  or maple syrup
whipped cream (optional)

1 Put the milk, dried fruit, orange peel and the cinnamon stick in a large, heavy-based saucepan and set over medium heat. Bring to a simmer and stir in the rice.

2 Reduce the heat to low and cook, stirring frequently to avoid scorching, for about 20 minutes, until the rice is tender and the mixture creamy.

3 Stir in the cream, sugar, vanilla extract, and salt and continue cooking for about 10 minutes longer, until the rice is completely tender and the mixture thick and creamy.

4 Pour the rice pudding into a large bowl and allow to cool to room temperature, stirring occasionally. Sprinkle with cinnamon sugar or brown sugar, or drizzle with maple syrup and serve with whipped cream, if using.

Orange-Scented French Toast

Serves 4

During the late 1960s, this sweetly old-fashioned breakfast dish was a popular way of using leftover stale bread. However, by using grated orange peel, you turn it into something more exotic, and he'll love that.

4 eggs
1 1/2 cups/375ml milk
grated peel and juice of 1/2 orange
1 tbsp sugar
1/3 cup/100g mild orange marmalade
  (optional)
8 slices egg brioche or challah bread,
  or thick white toasting bread
1/4 cup/60g butter
orange blossom honey, maple syrup,
  or marmalade, to serve

1 Put the eggs in a large, shallow bowl and beat lightly. Add the milk, orange peel and juice, sugar, and marmalade, if using, and whisk until well blended.

2 Dip each slice of bread in the egg mixture, turning to coat all over and allow the bread to absorb the mixture. Transfer the bread to a large baking sheet. Slowly pour over any remaining egg mixture and allow to stand for 5–10 minutes until all the mixture has soaked in.

3 Melt half the butter in a large frying pan over medium heat. Working in two batches, carefully add four bread slices in a single layer and cook for 5–7 minutes, turning once, until golden on both sides. Transfer to a warm plate and cook the remaining slices. Serve drizzled with honey or maple syrup, or with marmalade.

New England Blueberry Pancakes

Serves 4–6

Bring back wonderful childhood memories by serving these heartwarming pancakes for a winter's breakfast. As an extra treat, serve with crispy bacon or breakfast sausages and just watch his face light up.

1¼ cups/ 150g all-purpose (plain) flour
½ tsp baking powder
½ tsp baking soda (bicarbonate of soda)
¼ tsp salt
1 cup/ 250ml buttermilk
¾ cup/ 185ml milk
1 tbsp sugar or honey
2 tbsp/ 25g butter, melted
½ tsp vanilla extract
½ cup/ 120g fresh blueberries
melted butter or vegetable oil, for frying
butter and maple syrup or honey,
  to serve

1 In a bowl, combine the flour, baking powder, baking soda, and salt, and make a well in the middle.

2 In another bowl, whisk together the buttermilk, about ½ cup/125ml of the milk, the sugar or honey, melted butter, and vanilla. Pour into the well and, using a whisk or fork, stir gently until just combined with the dry mixture. If the batter is too thick, add a little more milk so that is can be poured. Do not overbeat—a few floury lumps do not matter. Gently fold in the blueberries.

3 Heat a large frying pan or pancake griddle (preferably nonstick) over medium heat and brush with melted butter or vegetable oil. Drop the batter in small ladlefuls on to the hot surface and cook until the edges are set and the surface bubbles begin to break, about 1 minute.

4 Turn each pancake and cook until just golden underneath, about 30 seconds longer. Transfer to a baking sheet and keep warm in a low oven until all the batter is cooked.

5 Serve hot with butter and maple syrup or honey.

Summer Berry Shortcakes

This dessert celebrates summer's lavish harvest of strawberry and other berries. Serve it with lashings of whipped cream.

Makes 8

1½lb/675g (about 6 cups) fresh ripe
  strawberries & other summer berries,
  hulled and sliced
2–3 tbsp superfine (caster) sugar
1–2 tbsp raspberry juice or 1 tbsp
  orange juice
2 cups/225g all-purpose (plain) flour
2½ tsp baking powder
½ tsp salt
2 tbsp sugar, plus extra for sprinkling
6 tbsp/90g unsalted butter, diced
1 cup/250ml heavy (double) or whipping
  cream, whipped to soft peaks and chilled
confectioners' (icing) sugar, for dusting
mint leaves, to decorate

1 Put the berries in a large bowl and toss with the superfine sugar and fruit juice. Leave to stand until the juices begin to run, stirring occasionally.

2 Preheat the oven to 425°F (220°C/Gas 7) and grease a baking sheet. Stir together the flour, baking powder, salt, and sugar in a large bowl. Add the butter and, using a pastry blender or your fingertips, rub it into the flour mixture until coarse crumbs form. Using a fork, lightly stir in all but 1 tablespoon of the cream, little by little, to make a soft dough.

3 Turn the dough out on to a lightly floured work surface and knead 6–8 times, until smooth. Pat or roll the dough into a rectangle about ½in/1cm thick. Using a round cutter, stamp out 8 rounds or, if you prefer, cut into eight 3in/7.5cm squares. Arrange 3in/7.5cm apart on the baking sheet. Brush the tops with the remaining cream and sprinkle with sugar.

4 Bake until set and the tops are pale golden, about 10 minutes. Transfer the shortcakes to a wire rack to cool.

5 Using a fork or serrated knife, split the shortcakes horizontally in half. Place the bottoms on 8 dessert plates and spoon the berries over them, reserving some for decoration. Spoon the chilled whipped cream over the berries. Place the shortcake tops on the cream, and decorate with a sliced berry. Dust with the confectioners' sugar and decorate each with a mint leaf.

Hot Fudge Sundae

A real soda fountain treat, this will take him right back to his carefree bachelor days. The story goes that the name sundae is derived from the fact that these ice cream treats were originally served only on Sunday, the Sabbath, as they contained no soda water, a mix associated with alcohol.

choice of ice cream, such as chocolate
   or vanilla fudge swirl
whipped cream, to serve
chocolate shavings, to decorate

Hot Fudge Sauce
1 cup/225g sugar
1 cup/250ml heavy (double) or
   whipping cream
2 tbsp/30g butter, cut up
1 tbsp light corn (golden) syrup
4oz/120g unsweetened (dark plain)
   chocolate, chopped
1 tsp vanilla extract

1 To prepare the sauce, put the sugar, cream, butter, syrup, and chocolate in a heavy-based saucepan and set over medium-high heat. Bring to a boil, stirring constantly, until the chocolate has melted and the mixture is smooth.

2 Reduce the heat to medium-low and cook for about 5 minutes, stirring frequently. Remove from the heat, stir in the vanilla extract and keep warm.

3 Place 2 scoops of ice cream in each of two scallop-edged sundae glasses or any dessert bowl. Spoon over 2 tablespoons fudge sauce, or to taste, and top with a swirl of whipped cream. Sprinkle with chocolate shavings and serve immediately.

Deluxe Banana Split

This is one of those desserts that is just too luscious for words and every dining table falls silent after the first "oohs" and "aahs" as the ice cream concoctions are served with aplomb.

Serves 2

2 ripe bananas
2 scoops each vanilla, chocolate, and
  strawberry ice cream
1/2 cup/125ml whipping cream, whipped
  and chilled
1/3 cup/40g chopped pecan nuts
2 maraschino cherries, drained

Fudge Sauce
1 cup/225g sugar
1 cup/250ml whipping or heavy
  (double) cream
1 tbsp light corn (golden) syrup
4oz/120g unsweetened (bitter plain)
  chocolate, chopped
2 tbsp butter, diced
1 tsp vanilla extract

Hot Butterscotch Sauce
1 cup/200g light brown sugar
1/2 cup/250ml whipping or heavy
  (double) cream
2 tbsp light corn (golden) syrup
1 tsp rum extract

1 Prepare the fudge sauce: cook the sugar, cream, corn syrup, and unsweetened chocolate in a medium, heavy-based saucepan over medium-high heat, stirring frequently, until the chocolate is melted and the sauce boils. Reduce the heat and stir in the butter and vanilla extract until smooth. Keep warm or allow to cool to room temperature.

2 Prepare the hot butterscotch sauce: put the brown sugar, cream, and light corn syrup in a saucepan and bring to a boil over medium-high heat. Boil for 2 minutes, then reduce the heat. Beat in the butter and simmer 2 minutes longer, until thickened. Stir in the rum extract and remove from the heat; cover and keep warm.

3 Soften the three ice creams to room temperature, if necessary, for about 5 minutes. Peel the bananas and split each one in half along its length. Lay 2 halves in each dish, forming a V–shape. Arrange a scoop of each ice cream along each split banana. Spoon a little of the fudge sauce over the chocolate and strawberry ice creams, and spoon the butterscotch sauce over the vanilla.

4 Pipe or spoon whipped cream over the ice cream, sprinkle with chopped pecans, and top with a cherry. Serve the extra sauces separately.

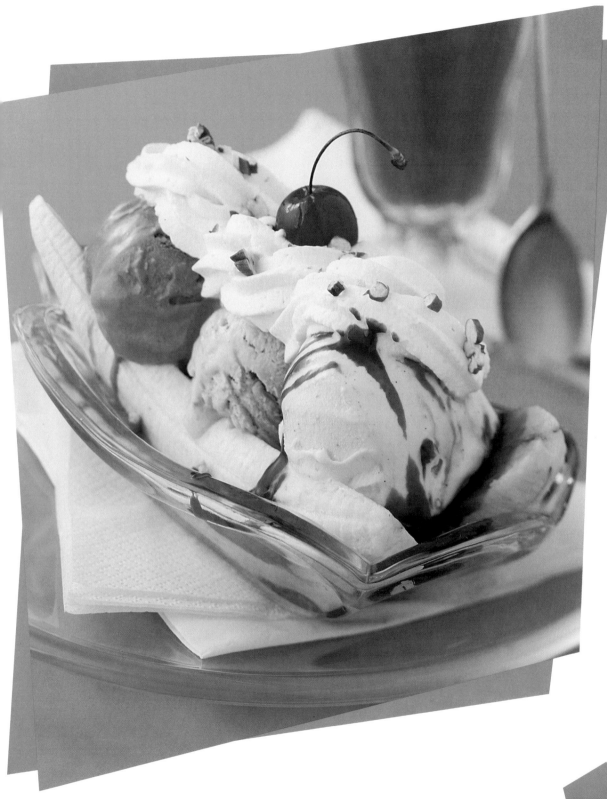

Chocolate Chunk Brownies

Add generous scoops of vanilla ice cream or luscious whipped cream to these melt-in-the-mouth brownies. They were the rave dessert of the 1930s and '40s, and they have never been abandoned by chocoholics. While few men own up to a weakness for fluffy sponge cake, many will happily admit to a weakness for gooey brownies.

3/4 cup/175g butter
4oz/120g unsweetened (bitter plain) chocolate, chopped
1 3/4 cups/400g sugar
3 eggs
1 1/3 cups/175g all-purpose (plain) flour
1 1/2 tsp vanilla extract
1/2 tsp salt
6oz/175g good quality semisweet (plain) chocolate, chopped
1/2 cup/50g chopped pecan nuts or walnuts

1 Preheat the oven to 350°F (180°C/Gas 4). Lightly grease a 13 x 9in/33 x 23cm nonstick baking pan. In a heavy-based saucepan, melt the butter and unsweetened chocolate over low heat, stirring frequently. Remove from the heat and stir in the sugar until dissolved; set aside to cool slightly.

2 Add the eggs one at a time, beating well after each addition. Stir in the flour, vanilla extract, and salt until just blended. Gently fold in the chopped chocolate and nuts but do not over-mix. Spread the batter evenly in the pan, pushing it into the corners.

3 Bake for 25–30 minutes, until the mixture is set and shiny on top. A cake tester or toothpick inserted into the middle should come out with a few wet crumbs still attached; do not over-bake. Leave to cool completely in the pan, then cut into 2in/5cm squares.

Peanut Butter Brownies

Makes 12–16

Keep these hidden in the cookie jar. He'll have a hard time trying to resist them! Chocolate and peanut butter are a classic American combination and it works really well in this fudgy brownie.

6oz/175g unsweetened (dark plain) chocolate
1 cup/225g butter
2 cups/450g sugar
4 eggs, lightly beaten
2 tsp vanilla extract
1/2 cup/50g all-purpose (plain) flour
1/2 tsp salt
1 cup/175g chocolate chips

PEANUT CRUNCH

PEANUT BUTTER

Peanut Butter Layer

1¼ cups/275g smooth peanut butter
½ cup/120g butter, softened
¼–½ cup/30–60g confectioners' (icing)
* sugar, plus extra for dusting*
6oz/175g honey roasted peanuts or white
* chocolate chips*

1 Mold a piece of aluminum foil over the bottom of an 8in/20cm square baking pan, then line the baking pan with the foil mold, pressing it into the corners and smoothing it out evenly.

2 Melt the chocolate and butter in a saucepan over medium-low heat, stirring frequently, until smooth. Remove from the heat and add the sugar, then stir until the sugar dissolves. Beat in the eggs, then stir in the vanilla, flour, salt, and chocolate chips until just blended— do not over-mix.

3 Spoon half the batter into the pan and spread evenly into the corners. Freeze for 15–20 minutes until the surface is firm. Cover the remaining mixture and set aside at room temperature.

4 Preheat the oven to 350°F (180°C/Gas 4). Put the peanut butter and butter in a large bowl and, using an electric beater, beat for about 2 minutes, until smooth and creamy. Beat in the confectioners' sugar and peanuts or white chocolate chips. Drip tablespoonfuls of the peanut mixture over the chocolate layer, then gently spread it evenly to make a smooth layer. Cover with the remaining chocolate mixture in the same way.

5 Bake for about 35 minutes, until the surface is puffed and set. Leave the mixture in the pan to cool completely. Using the foil as a guide, lift the brownie out of the pan and set it on a work surface. Dust with a little confectioners' sugar before cutting into squares or bars.

Angel Food Cake

Serves 12–16

This lightest of sponge cakes has been widely popular since the late 1800s, when it was probably made by frugal cooks to use up surplus egg whites. It will remind your man of mother's special-occasion cooking and dinner party desserts.

1½ cups/ 175g confectioners' (icing) sugar
1 cup/ 120g cake (sponge), pastry, or all-
   purpose (plain) flour
1½ cups/ 375ml egg white
   (about 12 large whites)
1½ tsp cream of tartar
1 tsp vanilla extract
¼ tsp salt
1 cup/ 165g superfine (caster) sugar

Raspberry Sauce

10oz/ 275g fresh or frozen raspberries
1 tbsp lemon juice
2 tbsp superfine (caster) sugar
1 tbsp raspberry preserves (jam)
2 tbsp raspberry liqueur

1 Preheat the oven to 350°F (180°C/Gas 4). Sift the confectioners' sugar and flour into a bowl and stir, then sift again. Set aside.

2 In a large bowl, whisk the egg whites, cream of tartar, vanilla extract, and salt with an electric mixer until soft peaks form. Gradually add the superfine sugar, 2 tablespoons at a time, and continue whisking until stiff peaks form.

3 Sift a quarter of the flour mixture over the whites and fold it in gently using a metal spoon. Repeat in three more batches until all the flour is added. Spoon the mixture gently into an ungreased angel food cake pan or 10in/25cm tube pan (ring tin).

4 Bake until risen, golden and the surface feels springy when gently pressed. Invert the cake pan and cool for 10 minutes. (An angel food pan has little feet to keep it off the work surface. If using a tube pan, invert it over the neck of a bottle to raise it off the work surface.) Gently loosen the cake from the pan edge and invert it on to a plate, then dust with sugar.

5 To prepare the raspberry sauce: put the raspberries, lemon juice, sugar, and preserves in a food processor and pulse until smooth. Strain into a bowl and stir in the liqueur. Chill. Serve the sauce with slices of the cake.

Dark Chocolate Layer Cake

When packaged mixes became widely available in the 1950s, everyone was making instant cakes. But you can treat him to the real thing instead, as it is just as easy to make this delicious, fudge-filled layer cake from scratch.

Serves 8–10

2 cups/225g all-purpose (plain) flour
1½ tsp baking soda (bicarbonate of soda)
½ tsp baking powder
1 tsp salt
1½ cups/350g sugar
2 tsp vanilla extract
1¼ cups/300ml buttermilk
½ cup/120g white vegetable shortening
  (white vegetable fat)
3 eggs
3oz/75g unsweetened (dark plain) chocolate,
  melted and cooled
chocolate curls, to decorate (optional)

Very Fudgy Frosting

2 cups/250ml heavy (double) cream
1lb/450g good-quality semisweet (plain) or
  bittersweet (dark bitter) chocolate, chopped
1/3 cup/75g unsalted butter, at room
  temperature
1 tbsp vanilla extract

1 Preheat the oven to 350°F (180°C/Gas 4). Grease and flour two 9in/23cm cake pans.

2 Make the cake by the all-in-one method: sift the flour, baking soda, baking powder, and salt into a large mixing bowl. Add the sugar, vanilla, buttermilk, shortening, eggs, and cooled melted chocolate. Using an electric beater on low speed, begin to beat the mixture slowly until the ingredients are well blended. Scrape the side of the bowl occasionally. Increase the mixer speed to high and beat for 5 minutes, scraping down the side of the bowl occasionally.

3 Divide the batter between the pans, smooth the tops evenly and bake for about 25 minutes, until the tops of the cakes are set. A toothpick (cocktail stick) inserted in the middle should come out with just one or two crumbs attached—do not over-bake the cakes or they will be dry. Leave to cool in the pans for 10 minutes, then turn out on to wire racks, turn the cakes right sides up, and leave to cool completely.

4 To make the frosting, pour the cream into a saucepan and bring to a boil over medium-high heat. Remove from the heat and add the chocolate, stirring until melted and smooth. Then beat in the butter and vanilla. Chill

to cool, stirring every 10–15 minutes, until the frosting becomes quite thick and spreadable. Remove from the refrigerator and continue to stir occasionally until the frosting is thick.

5 Place one cake layer, top side up, on a plate and spread with about a quarter of the frosting. Cover with the second layer, flat side up and coat the top and sides of the cake, making deep swirls with a palette knife or the back of a spoon. Decorate with chocolate curls, if using.

COOK'S TIP
For a four-layer cake, split the two layers horizontally and frost between each layer, ending with the last layer flat side up. Then frost the top and sides as above.

Blueberry Coffeecake with Streusel Topping

People all over the world love the traditional sweet breads and cakes, introduced by German and Dutch immigrants. Coffeecake is the classic breakfast treat, served warm with lots of aromatic fresh coffee—what a nice way to start a weekend together!

Serves 8–10

Topping

1/2 cup/120g butter, softened
2/3 cup/150g sugar
1/3 packed cup/45g light brown sugar
2/3 cup/65g all-purpose (plain) flour
1/2 cup/50g chopped toasted walnuts or
   pecan nuts
1 1/2 tsp ground cinnamon
1/2 tsp grated nutmeg
1/2 tsp salt

Filling

12oz/350g cream cheese, softened
1/3 cup/65g sugar
1 egg
grated peel of 1 lemon
1–2 tbsp lemon juice
1 tsp vanilla extract

Cake

4 cups/450g all-purpose (plain) flour
4 tsp baking powder
1 tsp salt
1/2 cup/120g butter, softened
1 1/4 cups/200g superfine sugar
2 eggs, lightly beaten
1 1/2 tsp vanilla extract
1 1/4 cups/300ml milk
3 cups/350g fresh blueberries

1 Preheat the oven to 375°F (190°C/Gas 5). Generously butter a 13 x 9in/33 x 23cm glass baking dish. Prepare the topping: in a bowl, rub together the butter, sugars, and flour to form large crumbs. Stir in the nuts, cinnamon, nutmeg, and salt. Chill until ready to use.

2 For the filling, beat the cream cheese until creamy using an electric mixer. Gradually beat in the sugar. Beat in the egg, lemon peel, juice, and vanilla extract. Set aside.

3 For the cake: sift the flour, baking powder, and salt into a bowl. In another bowl, beat the butter with an electric mixer until creamy. Gradually beat in the sugar until the mixture is fluffy. Then beat in

the eggs and vanilla extract. On low speed, beat in the flour alternately with the milk to blend well. Fold in the blueberries.

4 Spread a little less than half the cake mixture in the bottom of the dish. Gently spread the cream cheese filling evenly over the cake mixture, then sprinkle a quarter of the streusel topping over the filling. Drop spoonfuls of the remaining cake mixture over the top and spread evenly. Sprinkle with the remaining topping.

5 Bake the coffeecake until crunchy and golden on top, about 1 hour. Leave to cool until warm, then cut into squares, and serve warm or at room temperature.

Chocolate-Chip Muffins

Raise his spirits with the heart-warming aroma of fresh baking. Muffins are classic 'quick breads' designed to be easy and failsafe. Forget packet mixes and bought breads—once sampled, these homemade muffins are must-have breads for breakfasts, teas and snacks.

Makes 10

1¾ cups/400g all-purpose (plain) flour
¼ cup/25g unsweetened cocoa powder
1 tbsp baking powder
½ tsp salt
½ cup/75g superfine (caster) sugar
⅔ cup/120g semisweet (plain)
  chocolate chips
2 eggs
½ cup/125ml sunflower or light
  vegetable oil
1 cup/250ml milk
1 tsp vanilla extract

Deluxe Peanut Butter Cookies

Makes 14—16

Stock your cookie jar with these toothsome treats—and hide them from your hungry male! Peanut butter was created in 1890 and is the ultimate 'good for you' snack. These cookies are simple to make and delicious to eat—too good to resist!

1 cup/150g shelled peanuts
vegetable oil, for greasing
1 cup/120g all-purpose (plain) flour
½ tsp baking soda (bicarbonate of soda)
¼ tsp salt
½ cup/120g butter, softened
½ cup/120g crunchy peanut butter
½ packed cup/75g light brown sugar
2 tbsp sugar
1 egg, beaten
1 tsp vanilla extract
5oz/150g white or semisweet (plain)
  chocolate, coarsely chopped

1 Roast the peanuts in a dry pan over medium heat, shaking and stirring until lightly and evenly browned. Transfer to a plate and leave to cool.

2 Preheat the oven to 375°F (190°C/Gas 5) and grease two baking sheets. Sift the flour, baking soda, and salt into a bowl. In a separate bowl, beat the butter and peanut butter together until creamy. Then beat in the brown sugar and sugar until the mixture is soft and fluffy.

3 Add the egg and vanilla, and beat into the creamed mixture. Add the flour mixture, peanuts and chocolate and stir until the ingredients are thoroughly combined.

4 Drop heaped tablespoons of the mixture 2in/5cm apart on to the prepared baking sheets. Moisten the bottom of a glass with water and use to flatten each heap of mixture, rinsing under cold water occasionally to prevent the mixture from sticking to the glass.

1 Preheat the oven to 400°F (200°C/Gas 6). Line 10 muffin-pan cups with double paper liners. Sift the flour, cocoa powder, baking powder, and salt into a bowl. Sift again, then stir in the sugar and chocolate chips. Make a well in the middle.

2 In another bowl, beat the eggs with the oil until foamy. Gradually beat in the milk and vanilla extract. Pour into the well in the flour mixture, and stir until just combined.

3 Spoon the batter into the paper liners. Bake until risen, well browned, and spongy, about 20 minutes. Leave to stand for about 10 minutes, then transfer to a wire rack to cool. Serve at room temperature.

COOK'S TIP
Half fill any empty muffin pan cups with water to prevent scorching.

5 Bake the cookies, one baking sheet at a time, for 10 minutes, until risen, spread and browned. Do not overbake. Allow to cool and firm up slightly on the sheet for 4 minutes, then transfer to a wire rack and leave to cool completely. Repeat with the remaining cookies and mixture, regreasing the baking sheets between batches. Store the cookies in an airtight container when completely cold.

COOK'S TIP
To 'recycle' a baking sheet when baking in batches, run it under cold water to cool. Dry and re-grease if necessary, ready for the next batch.

Chocolate Chip Cookies

Makes about 35 large cookies

The popular obsession with chocolate chip cookies took off when chocolate chips first became widely available in the 1950s. The original recipe for Toll-House Cookies on the back of the yellow package of Nestle's chocolate chips cannot be bettered, except maybe by adding a little extra chocolate!

2¹/₂ cups/250g all-purpose (plain) flour
1 tsp baking soda (bicarbonate of soda)
¹/₂ tsp salt
³/₄ cup/6oz butter, softened
2 tbsp/25g white vegetable shortening
  (white vegetable fat)
1 packed cup/75g light brown sugar
¹/₂ cup/120g sugar
2 eggs, lightly beaten
2 tsp vanilla extract
12oz/350g semisweet (plain) chocolate chips
1 cup/175g white chocolate chips (optional)
1 cup/100g chopped pecan nuts or walnuts
  (optional)

1 Preheat the oven to 375°F (190°C/Gas 5). Lightly grease two large heavy baking sheets.

2 Sift the flour, baking soda and salt into a bowl; set aside. Using an electric beater, beat the butter and shortening in a large bowl until blended. Add the light brown and ordinary sugars and beat until fluffy, about 2 minutes. Gradually beat in the eggs and vanilla until smooth.

3 Add the flour mixture in two or three batches and beat into the butter mixture on low speed until it is well blended. Stir in the chocolate chips and the nuts, if using.

4 Drop heaped tablespoonfuls of the mixture 2in/5cm apart on to the baking sheets. Bake for 8–10 minutes, until golden and set around the edges. Leave to cool slightly on the baking sheets, then transfer to a wire rack to cool completely.

141

Philadelphia Breakfast Buns

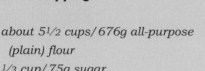

Makes 15

Philadelphia is famous for these finger-licking breakfast buns, an old specialty from the nearby Pennsylvania Dutch community. The delicious yeast rolls are filled with fruit and nuts and coated with a sticky brown sugar and butter topping.

about 5¹/2 cups/676g all-purpose (plain) flour
1/3 cup/75g sugar
1 tsp salt
1 tbsp active dry yeast (easy-blend dried yeast)
1¹/2 cups/375ml water
1 cup/225g butter
1 egg

Filling and Topping

1 cup/75g packed dark brown sugar
1/2 cup/125ml dark corn (golden) syrup
1 cup/125g pecan nuts, chopped
1/2 cup/60g raisins or currants
1 tsp ground cinnamon

1 Put 2 cups/250g of the flour into a large bowl and stir in the sugar, salt and dry yeast, then make a well in the middle of these dry ingredients.

2 In a small saucepan, heat the water and half the butter over medium-low heat until just warm, 120–130°F/50–55°C. Using an electric mixer, gradually beat the warm water and butter mixture into the dry ingredients until just blended. Increase the speed to medium and beat for 2 minutes, scraping down the side of the bowl occasionally.

3 Beat in the egg and another 1 cup/120g flour until a thick batter forms, and beat for 2 minutes more. Using a wooden spoon, stir in 2¹/4 cups/275g more flour until a soft dough forms.

4 Turn the dough out on to a well-floured surface and knead until smooth and elastic, working in about 1/4 cup/30g more flour—this should take about 10 minutes.

5 Grease a large bowl with a little oil. Shape the dough into a ball and place it in the bowl, then turn it over so that the top of the dough is greased. Cover with a clean dish towel or plastic wrap (cling film) and leave to rise in a warm place until the dough has doubled in volume, 1 1/2–2 hours.

6 Heat the brown sugar, syrup, and remaining butter in a saucepan over medium-high heat until boiling, reduce the heat to low and simmer for about 3 minutes. Pour about 1/2 cup/125ml of the melted mixture into a small bowl and stir in the pecans, raisins or currants, and cinnamon; set aside. Lightly grease a 13 x 9in/33 x 23cm pan (baking tin) and pour in the remaining mixture, spreading it evenly.

7 Punch down the dough and turn it on to a lightly floured surface, cover with the upturned bowl and leave to rest for 15 minutes. Roll out the dough into a 15 x 13in/37.5 x 32.5cm rectangle and spread the fruit and nut filling over.

8 Starting with one long edge, roll up the dough tightly, as for jelly (Swiss) roll, then roll seam side down and press gently to seal. Cut into 15 slices and place these, cut-side down, evenly apart in the prepared pan. Cover with a tea towel and allow to rise in a warm place until doubled in volume, about 45 minutes. Preheat the oven to 375°F (190°C/Gas 5).

9 Bake the buns until they are well browned and the syrup is bubbling, about 30 minutes. Invert the pan on to a large foil-lined baking sheet and leave to stand, allowing the syrup to drip over the buns. Carefully remove the pan. Separate the buns and serve warm. Alternatively, reheat in the oven, wrapped in foil, if serving them later.

Index

Picture Credits

Look! Conversion tables
P.S. only use one system at a time!

Liquid Measures

¼ tsp	=	1.25ml
½ tsp	=	2.5ml
1 tsp	=	5ml
2 tsp	=	10ml
1 tbsp	=	15ml
2 fl oz	=	60ml
4 fl oz	=	125ml
5 fl oz	=	150ml
6 fl oz	=	185ml
8 fl oz	=	250ml
½ pt	=	300ml
13 fl oz	=	375ml
14 fl oz	=	400ml
¾ pt	=	450ml
18 fl oz	=	500ml
1 pt	=	600ml
1¼ pints	=	750ml
1¾ pints	=	1 litre
2 pints	=	1.2 litres
2½ pints	=	1.5 litres
3½ pints	=	2 litres

Dry Measures

¼oz	=	10g	8oz	=	225g
½oz	=	15g	9oz	=	250g
¾oz	=	20g	10oz	=	275g
1oz	=	25g	11oz	=	300g
1½oz	=	40g	12oz	=	350g
2oz	=	50g	14oz	=	400g
2½oz	=	65g	15oz	=	425g
3oz	=	75g	1lb	=	450g
3½oz	=	90g	1¼lb	=	500g
4oz	=	115g	1½lb	=	675g
4½oz	=	130g	2lb	=	900g
5oz	=	150g	2¼lb	=	1kg
5½oz	=	165g	3–3½lb	=	1.5kg
6oz	=	175g	4–4½lb	=	1.75kg
6½oz	=	185g	5–5¼lb	=	2.25kg
7oz	=	200g	6lb	=	2.75kg

Butter

			⅓ cup	=	75g
			½ cup	=	120g
1 tbsp	=	15g	⅔ cup	=	150g
2 tbsp	=	25g	¾ cup	=	175g
3 tbsp	=	45g	1 cup	=	225g
4 tbsp	=	55g	1½ cups	=	350g
5 tbsp	=	75g	1 stick	=	115g
6 tbsp	=	90g	1½ sticks	=	175g
			3 sticks	=	350g